THE WORLD OF
VANITY FAIR

SPHERE

First published in Great Britain in 2018 by Sphere
Vanity Fair™ © 2018 Mammoth Screen Limited
Text Copyright © Little, Brown Book Group 2018
Editorial by Emma Marriott / Tall Tree Limited and Sphere
All rights reserved.

A CIP catalogue record for this book
is available from the British Library.

ISBN 978-0-7515-7424-1

Designed by Sian Rance for D.R. ink
Printed and bound in Italy by L.E.G.O. S.p.A.
Papers used by Sphere are from well-managed forests and other responsible sources.

Sphere
An imprint of
Little, Brown Book Group
Carmelite House
50 Victoria Embankment
London EC4Y 0DZ

An Hachette UK Company
www.hachette.co.uk

www.littlebrown.co.uk

THE WORLD OF
VANITY FAIR

EMMA MARRIOTT

FOREWORD BY
MICHAEL PALIN

CONTENTS

✗

FOREWORD

by Michael Palin

MANY YEARS AGO I was a castaway on *Desert Island Discs*, then presented by Roy Plomley. Like all guests, I was invited to choose eight recordings, a book and a luxury item to take with me. My chosen recordings ranged from part of a comedy sketch by the Goons to music by Elvis, Duke Ellington and Edward Elgar, and my luxury item was a feather pillow, preferably with a bed. And for my chosen book? Well, it had to be *Vanity Fair*.

The reasons I gave then still hold today: *Vanity Fair* is full of humour, insight and jollity, and I could envisage being endlessly entertained by it on my lonely desert island. When I first read *Vanity Fair*, it really stood out from other classic English novels, mainly because of the mischievousness of the heroine, Becky Sharp. I was also drawn to the satirist that is William Thackeray; the way he takes people apart, debunks pomposity and pretentiousness wherever he finds it, while at the same time creating a heroine who is completely unscrupulous. I really like that contrast and it's such a bracing story to read – and was very different from anything else I had read at that time.

I read *Vanity Fair* at about the same time as I was working on *Monty Python* and I enjoyed the spirit of anarchy in the book, the feeling that Thackeray is trying to stir things up but also control everything at the same time. Much of the novel's brilliance comes down to the liveliness of his creation Becky Sharp, and the way she cuts through the dreadful world of *Vanity Fair*, not as a saint by any means, but as somebody who knows how to operate.

As a result, when Gwyneth Hughes asked me to play Thackeray, I was so pleased to take on the role. Gwyneth felt that Thackeray should appear at the beginning and end of the story, because *Vanity Fair* is very much his book, it's his property and he's at the helm – although at times it feels that Becky is the one in control! His appearances at the beginning and end of each episode convey the idea that he has ownership over the characters, which bits of the story he wants to emphasise and the mischief he (and they) get up to in the process.

For me, *Vanity Fair* is about people behaving in a very self-satisfied way; it's about money and all that it can buy you; it's about the way you look and the way you are, and your name rather than what you're actually saying or what's going on in your mind. It's about human vanity, the eternal idea that if we look like this or do that then we'll be better people. Thackeray says no, that's all a charade – and that's what is so appealing about Becky, because, despite being manipulative and scheming, she is a real character; in fact, the strongest character in a world of fools.

So I'm very happy to have come full circle, to return to *Vanity Fair* and to stand in for William Thackeray: it's a real honour. And if I were to be asked back to *Desert Island Discs*, I've no doubt my chosen book would remain the same. There are so many insightful and entertaining passages in the book, but the following rings as true now as it did for me many years ago, and is testament to the enduring appeal of *Vanity Fair* and to the genius of its creator:

The world is a looking-glass, and gives back to every man the reflection of his own face. Frown at it, and it will in turn look sourly upon you; laugh at it and with it, and it is a jolly kind companion …

As the Manager of the Performance

sits before the curtain on the boards, and looks into

the Fair, a feeling of profound melancholy comes over

him in his survey of the bustling place. There is a great

quantity of eating and drinking, making love and

jilting, laughing and the contrary, smoking, cheating,

fighting, dancing and fiddling: there are bullies pushing

about, bucks ogling the women, knaves picking pockets,

policemen on the look-out …

Please remember that my story has Vanity

Fair *for a title and that Vanity Fair is a very*

vain, wicked, foolish place, full of all sorts of

humbug and falseness and pretension. Not

a moral place, certainly, nor a merry one,

though VERY NOISY

is striving for what is not

worth having

THE WORLD OF *Vanity Fair* teems with life. Everyone is on the make, trying to survive, to get on, or to cling to what they have. Envy, ambition, self-regard and pretension lurk in every drawing room, servants' kitchen or gentlemen's club. Those who have little have further to climb, but everyone is striving for something: social standing, riches, pleasures, or what they think will make them happy.

This 'wicked, foolish place' is England in 1813. It's a seething, turbulent society that has been embroiled in war for twenty years; old money mixes with new in an expanding and changing economy; people become rich and some starve; a growing empire brings new opportunities; foolish men gamble away their fortunes; and women are expected to behave in a manner thought proper to their station.

At the helm of *Vanity Fair* is our author and narrator, William Makepeace Thackeray. He surveys the scene, piercing the elegant sheen of Regency life to reveal the sordid reality and beating heart beneath. It's a thrilling ride, a wild carousel that gets faster and faster, much to the delight of his young tenacious heroine, Becky Sharp. Dangerous as it is, she is a free spirit and

CHAPTER
ONE

Rebecca in the presence
of her enemy

---

*We thought her so exotic,
Mamma, with her wild hair,
and singing her little songs*

WE BEGIN OUR story at Miss Pinkerton's Academy for Young Ladies. Here, Miss Rebecca Sharp, a lowly teacher's apprentice, issues the headmistress, Miss Pinkerton, with an ultimatum: pay her properly or find her a station elsewhere. Miss Pinkerton calls her bluff and Becky is forced to pack up her meagre possessions. Kindly stockbroker's daughter Amelia Sedley takes pity on the poor orphan and offers to take her home for the week. Becky quickly makes herself at home at the Sedley house, where she targets Amelia's wealthy but oafish brother, Jos, and makes it her mission to charm him into proposing marriage.

Amelia persuades her snobbish fiancé, Lieutenant George Osborne, to take a party to the Vauxhall Pleasure Gardens. George brings his best friend, Captain William Dobbin, who is secretly in love with Amelia. At Vauxhall, Becky hangs on Jos's every word, but Jos drinks too much rack punch and makes a fool of himself. George ridicules his choice of an impoverished bride and scares Jos off. Becky must now leave the Sedley house and take up her position as governess at a run-down old mansion in Hampshire. Alone in the world again, Becky catches sight of Captain Rawdon Crawley, her new master's dashing younger son …

In search of happiness

IT IS REBECCA Sharp who takes centre stage in *Vanity Fair*. Her wit, cleverness and irreverence immediately set her apart from the pampered girls at Miss Pinkerton's Academy for Young Ladies. We soon learn that, unlike many of her fellow pupils, she is an orphan of 'low birth': her father was a drunkard artist and her mother an opera-girl. In lieu of school fees, Becky teaches music and French, the language of her mother, in which she is fluent.

We also meet Amelia Sedley. The daughter of a prosperous London stockbroker, Amelia is in sharp relief to Becky: sweet, delicate and often close to tears, and many at the school are sorry to see her go. These two young women, one well-born, gentle and submissive and the other from humble beginnings, spirited and fiercely independent, couldn't be more different. *Vanity Fair* is the tale of their parallel fortunes, the story of two girls as they journey through life, one in search of happiness and the other wanting 'tomorrow to be better than today'.

As the carriage takes Amelia and Becky away from Miss Pinkerton's, Becky hurls out of the window the dictionaries that were given to them by the school as leaving gifts. The gesture is significant and tells us a good deal about Becky.

While the moneyed pupils at Miss Pinkerton's are groomed to become ladies of leisure and to marry well, Becky, who lacks any sort of private income, has to make her own way in the world. For a poor girl like Becky, who had received a lady's education, there would have been few respectable employment options other than to become a teacher, either in a school like Pinkerton's or in a private house as a governess. The prospect of becoming a governess, however, is clearly not what Becky had imagined for herself: she is appalled at the very thought of it.

The dictionary in question is that of Samuel Johnson, first published in 1755 and revered as the pre-eminent English dictionary of the time. By ejecting it, Becky is spurning everything that such an esteemed volume represents: social order, male authority and a respect for precedent. We admire her audacity and see it as just revenge for Miss Pinkerton's condescending treatment of her low-born pupil. But it's also a callous gesture, a rejection of the well-meaning gift of Miss Pinkerton's sister, Jemima. In an instant we witness the complex nature of Becky, her bold, rebellious spirit and her propensity for wickedness, much to the consternation of her travelling companion.

MISS PINKERTON

Then I fear the real world will come as a dreadful shock to you.

BECKY

I'm the only girl under your roof who has the first idea what the real world is like.

Becky's knowledge of French adds to her worldliness and again marks her out as different from Amelia and the cosseted, more parochial girls around her. In celebration of her leaving the stifling world of Miss Pinkerton's, Becky exclaims '*Vive la France!*' and '*Vive Napoleon!*' as she enters the new and exciting world of London. As Britain has been mired in war against Napoleon and *la France* for the last twenty-three years, Becky is clearly out to shock. She, like Napoleon, is an upstart challenging the old order. The world is hers for the taking and she is going to use every weapon at her disposal – her natural cunning, intelligence and sexuality – to take it.

A magical carousel

VANITY FAIR OPENS with the captivating image of a carousel at night, which begins to spin at the finger-click of the fair-master standing before it. The overseer of the carousel is our narrator, William Makepeace Thackeray, and it is he who introduces us to the magical world of *Vanity Fair.*

Thackeray has a strong presence in the original novel: he introduces us to his world and his characters, and adds comments and asides throughout. The series creators similarly wanted Thackeray to feature in their adaptation, as director James Strong explains: 'The voice of Thackeray is very important to the story because it's his narration that holds the whole thing together. Thackeray described his role as a kind of puppet-master who controls the whole story.'

Gwyneth Hughes, the series writer and one of the executive producers, had the idea that Thackeray should appear at the beginning of each episode: 'I had the image in my mind of the young people on a carousel, but I knew that this would only work if we had Thackeray present, telling us what to think, that this is his story. But we had to think carefully about who this could be – who would the audience trust and love?'

The opening sequence is accompanied by the Bob Dylan track 'All Along the Watchtower'. 'The music at the beginning immediately announces this is a different retelling of *Vanity Fair*,' explains producer Julia Stannard. 'The song is all about discontent, disassociation and a world where values are inside out – it felt sympathetic to the story and an appropriate voice. Our version, which sits outside the drama, uses a modern, beautiful female voice and felt right for *Vanity Fair*.'

'Of course, there was only one person we wanted for Thackeray,' continues Gwyneth, 'and that was Michael Palin. He was thrilled to be asked and he was exactly right for the part. He has that twinkle in his eye, the sense that he's in control, he's telling the story, and you better listen because it's going to be fun – it's going to be a ride.'

To convey the dazzling lights and hypnotic feel of the carousel, the opening sequence was shot at night: 'The carousel is such an amazing prop – and to see it lit up in the mist at night really does create a magical feeling,' says Michael. 'I like the idea of the carousel as well. The characters go round and round, as that's what life is: it's a continuum, a continuous ride in which all the characters rise and fall towards their destinies.'

Carousels had been a part of English fairs since the eighteenth century. 'Gallopers' first appeared in the mid-1880s and quickly evolved into grand machines. They were originally steam-powered and would have had oil-based lamps, which were prone to catching fire – one of the reasons why many didn't survive. The carousel used in the opening sequence was built in 1893, and has been working ever since.

LEFT TO RIGHT: Director James Strong, Michael Palin, producer Julia Stannard.

MICHAEL PALIN: I quite enjoy night shoots because they concentrate the mind wonderfully. People get more work done in the last two hours of a night shoot because they realise time's running out and they want to get to bed.

REBECCA SHARP

OLIVIA COOKE PLAYS the unforgettable role of Rebecca Sharp. In her words: 'Becky Sharp is the ultimate manipulator, social climber, lover of fun and wealth, and she doesn't take life too seriously. She's an orphan, a survivor and she's out for number one.

'On top of that, she's incredibly intelligent and multi-faceted. She can play instruments, speak other languages, and she's constantly analysing people. Becky knows how men work and how to manipulate them and use her body. She's an attractive woman so she knows the effect she has on men. She has had to learn all of those things because she doesn't have a mother or father and she's trying to propel herself through society.'

Series writer Gwyneth Hughes agrees that once you've met Becky Sharp, it's difficult to forget her. 'She's the central character and driving force of *Vanity Fair*, but you couldn't describe her as a true heroine, as she behaves so badly! She's a vibrant, amoral, exciting character, and she doesn't always get it right.'

Casting the actress to play Becky was a huge decision for the series creators, as producer Julia Stannard explains: 'Becky is one of the great characters of English literature. She's a working-class girl from humble beginnings, and we wanted someone very real and vibrant, who had spirit and feistiness. Olivia was just perfect; she has her own thoughts on the character, she's very real, and we could see she had a lot of raw talent.'

Olivia relished playing the role of Becky and immersing herself in the world of *Vanity Fair*, a series that couldn't be more different from her previous roles, which include the television drama-thriller *Bates Motel* and, more recently, the lead female character, Art3mis, in Steven Spielberg's *Ready Player One*.

'There's always going to be elements of me in every character I play,' explains Olivia. 'Becky has taught me to be a lot more mischievous and naughty, which I think was always there, but has been pushed to the max in this job! However, when it comes to Becky's tenacity and blinkered view of the world I think I'd feel too much shame and guilt in living my life quite so selfishly as she does.'

Becky meets Amelia at Miss Pinkerton's and, much to the annoyance of the headmistress, arranges to spend a week with Amelia in London before taking up her position as governess in Hampshire. Becky is instinctively drawn to London and her head is turned by the Sedleys' fine Bloomsbury house – and Amelia's unattached (and rich) brother. As Olivia says, 'When Becky first sees Jos, she can't believe her luck, although all she cares about is his bank account. Here's this person who has been handed to her on a plate, who she can manipulate for her own gain. Others, however, quickly see through her and put the kibosh on that.'

Jos leaves, shattering Becky's dreams of marriage, but she simply moves on; she's not the type to brood on the past. And she realises that Amelia isn't really useful to her any more. 'Becky used to see Amelia as something to aspire to,' explains Olivia, 'until she realises that that way of life would ultimately be quite boring, and not enough for Becky, as she craves more and more.

'Becky's driving force is to ascend through society. She is mischievous, if she's down she's never down for long, she always has a plan, although her emotions don't really go too deep. She does have a heart, it's buried quite deep and it has lots of scars, due to her childhood, and having no one to look out for her. She has a defence mechanism, but it's excavated as her story goes on.'

When attacked sometimes, Becky had a knack of adopting a demure ingénue air, under which she was most dangerous. She said the wickedest things with the most simple unaffected air when in this mood, and would take care artlessly to apologize for her blunders, so that all the world should know that she had made them.

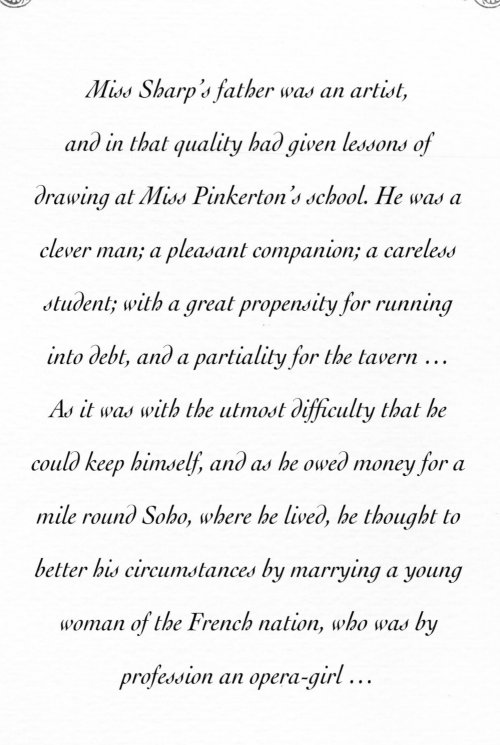

Miss Sharp's father was an artist,

and in that quality had given lessons of

drawing at Miss Pinkerton's school. He was a

clever man; a pleasant companion; a careless

student; with a great propensity for running

into debt, and a partiality for the tavern …

As it was with the utmost difficulty that he

could keep himself, and as he owed money for a

mile round Soho, where he lived, he thought to

better his circumstances by marrying a young

woman of the French nation, who was by

profession an opera-girl …

Miss Pinkerton, played by the English actress Suranne Jones.

One-shilling instalments

AS WITH MANY Victorian novels, *Vanity Fair* was first published in serial form; each of its nineteen instalments, from January 1847 to July 1848, sold for a shilling. Like Charles Dickens, who published all of his novels serially, beginning with *The Pickwick Papers* in 1836–7, authors tended to write their novels as they were being published. This gave writers an ongoing pressure to meet their monthly deadlines, and Thackeray was no exception: he frequently had to write at a tremendous pace and, like Dickens, missed the occasional deadline.

Monthly instalments created a particular relationship between author and reader, both of whom lived with the characters over a long period of time, with readers sometimes even writing to their favourite authors to try to influence the development of the narrative. Suspense was key, and novelists employed a variety of means to grip their readers from month to month, an element that only serves to make their novels real page-turners.

Even before the last of the instalments was published, *Vanity Fair* had been hailed as a literary treasure, although some criticised its darker portrayal of human weakness. Nonetheless, its success made Thackeray a name in fashionable society, with many viewing him as an equal of Dickens and his book as one of the greatest novels in the English language. He remained 'at the top of the tree', as he put it, for the rest of his life.

VANITY FAIR:

PEN AND PENCIL SKETCHES OF ENGLISH SOCIETY.

BY W. M. THACKERAY,

Author of "The Irish Sketch Book:" "Journey from Cornhill to Grand Cairo:" of "Jeames's Diary"
and the "Snob Papers" in "Punch:" &c. &c.

LONDON:

PUBLISHED AT THE PUNCH OFFICE, 85, FLEET STREET.

J. MENZIES, EDINBURGH; J. M'LEOD, GLASGOW; J. M'GLASHAN, DUBLIN.

1847.

[Bradbury & Evans, Printers, Whitefriars.]

Included in the monthly parts of *Vanity Fair* were numerous sketches and decorations drawn by Thackeray himself, which give an extra commentary on the storyline. These also appeared in the first complete book of *Vanity Fair*, published in 1848, with a revised edition in 1853 and many reprints since. Many of Thackeray's early writings and his letters are amusingly illustrated, and at one point he seriously considered taking up painting as a profession. Some, however, thought that Thackeray's artistic skills did not quite match his genius as a writer.

LEFT: Dobbin sees off onlookers who are fascinated by Jos's drunken courtship of Becky at Vauxhall Pleasure Gardens.

RIGHT: Becky meets Sir Pitt Crawley for the first time.

What's in a title

THE STORY OF *Vanity Fair* evolved out of 'Pen and Pencil Sketches of English Society', a series Thackeray had begun in 1844. When Thackeray first submitted the initial instalment of his novel to publishers, he had not yet called it 'Vanity Fair' – by the time of its publication by the *Punch* magazine proprietors Bradbury & Evans, he had settled on the title, although the subtitles 'Pen and Pencil Sketches of English Society' and 'Novel without a Hero' were used for the monthly instalments and first book publication respectively.

The *Vanity Fair* theme may have been in Thackeray's head since the 1830s, a result of visiting the studio of his friend George Cruikshank, the celebrated caricaturist and book illustrator, who had been commissioned to illustrate a new edition of John Bunyan's *The Pilgrim's Progress*. This book, first published in 1678, describes

Christian and Faithful pass through Vanity Fair: an illustration from *The Pilgrim's Progress*.

Rose and Violet with their mother, Lady Crawley. A daughter of an ironmonger, Lady Crawley thought she had won the lottery of life marrying Sir Pitt, but instead she is neglected and unloved, becoming a 'mere machine' in her husband's house. As is common in *Vanity Fair*, in the pursuit of personal gain, she has lost everything.

In the series, there is a nod to the origins of Vanity Fair, when the young pupils Rose and Violet are instructed by their uncle, Bute Crawley, to read *The Pilgrim's Progress*.

ROSE

Then I saw in my Dream, that when Christian and Faithful were got out of the Wilderness, they presently saw a Town before them …

VIOLET

And the name of that Town is Vanity; and at the Town there is a Fair kept called Vanity-Fair …

the pilgrimage of a hero named Christian, whose journey toward the Celestial City is beset by many perils. It is an allegory of man's spiritual journey through life, and the struggles and temptations we all face. In Bunyan's novel, 'Vanity Fair' is a place where people are entertained and goods are sold, a never-ending fair set up by devils to tempt pilgrims from the true path to salvation.

Many people in the 1840s would have been familiar with Bunyan's work, and the term 'Vanity Fair' was increasingly used to describe the world, or playground, of the idle and undeserving rich. Vanity Fair represents a society in which the desire for material wealth and pleasure exceeds all. This is the world that Thackeray's characters inhabit – a world in which no one looks beneath the surface, and where all kinds of vanities are on display.

The greatest event of history

THE CORE OF *Vanity Fair* is set in 1815, the year of the Battle of Waterloo, some thirty-two years before Thackeray published his novel. The author was looking back to an earlier period, reimagining what he called 'the greatest event of history' through the prism of his own times.

Much had changed. By the 1840s, Queen Victoria was on the throne, Britain was increasingly dominant overseas, with a burgeoning empire, and society was being transformed by the Industrial Revolution. The mentalities of the two periods were also quite different: while social hierarchy was very much present in the early nineteenth century, the rules that governed society, behaviour and

The marriage of Queen Victoria and Albert of Saxe-Coburg and Gotha, 10 February 1840.

etiquette were more fluid – much to the amusement of the strait-laced Victorians. As Dr Oskar Cox Jensen, one of the historical advisers on *Vanity Fair*, explains: 'To the Victorians, the Georgian and Regency period was a very different world, one of lust and disgrace with all sorts of things going on. Thackeray preserved that in his writing, with his larger-than-life characters and scandalous libertines; he imagines how the uncle whom no one speaks about or the wicked grandfather behaved. And whilst these were scandalous times, they were also very exciting times to a Victorian. Thackeray came from the Georgian tradition of satirists, like the caricatures of Gillray, Rowland and Cruikshank, who were famed for ribald, licentious but very sharp social criticism, and that's the tradition Thackeray is harking back to.'

By the early 1840s, Thackeray was mulling over the idea of writing about the Battle of Waterloo. The Napoleonic Wars were still very much in the public consciousness and Thackeray admitted he was fascinated by the deep-rooted national feeling that Waterloo had stirred for decades afterwards and how at the time the wars must have affected every part of society. Injured sailors and soldiers who had fought at Waterloo still haunted many of Britain's towns and cities, and the wars would prove fertile ground for writers in Britain and abroad, from Stendhal's *The Charterhouse of Parma* (1839) to Dickens's *Tale of Two Cities* (1859) and Tolstoy's *War and Peace* (1869).

MONSTROSITIES of 1819, & 182

The Duke of Wellington (see page 125), the conquering hero of Waterloo, was still very much a public figure in the 1840s, as an elder statesman in the Tory party and the leader of the House of Lords. In 1847, a military general service medal was issued to all surviving soldiers of the Peninsular War (see page 125) and there were permanent reminders of Waterloo everywhere, from the monument erected near Ancrum in the Scottish borders to Waterloo Bridge across the River Thames in London, and the equestrian statue of the Duke of Wellington mounted on the Wellington Arch opposite Apsley House, the Duke's London residence.

Thackeray had previously scorned patriotism ('the faith of the dullards'), and in his satirical poem 'The Chronicle of the Drum' ridiculed those who glorified 'the noble art of murdering'. But still, he was dogged by the thought that 'something might be made of Waterloo'. Having not had any military experience himself, in the end he chose to focus on the civilian events at the time of the battle, on human relationships and how adversity and violent hostility permeate everyday life.

At the same time, there were universal truths in the novel that spoke to people in the 1840s. In 1848, there were uprisings and revolutions across Europe, which resonated with the upheavals in the period after the French Revolution and during the Napoleonic Wars. In January that year, Abraham Hayward wrote in the *Edinburgh Review* that in *Vanity Fair*, 'the most stirring period is the Waterloo year, 1815 … The war fever was at its height: Napoleon was regarded as an actual monster: the belief that one Englishman could beat two Frenchmen, and ought to do it whenever he had an opportunity, was universal …'

In the text of *Vanity Fair*, Thackeray frequently expresses nostalgia for the early nineteenth century, a period of travel by stagecoach. By contrast, the 1840s saw huge growth in steam-powered rail transport, with railway lines built across the entire country. This spelled the end of the stagecoach, as Thackeray laments in the novel:

But the writer of these pages, who has pursued in former days, and in the same bright weather, the same remarkable journey, cannot but think of it with a sweet and tender regret. Where is the road now, and its merry incidents of life? ... Alas! we shall never hear the horn sing at midnight, or see the pike-gates fly open any more.

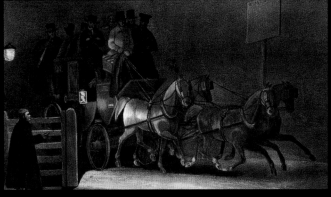

The setting

BUT LET US return to the start of the novel, to 1813 and the year in which we are first introduced to Becky, the Sedleys and the gallery of characters of *Vanity Fair*. Who was in government and on the throne, and what were the wars that had been raging in Europe?

In 1813, most people were unable to vote and politicians were largely drawn from the likes of Sir Pitt Crawley – the aristocracy and landed gentry – rather that the newly emerging business and professional classes. Throughout much of the period of *Vanity Fair*, from 1812 to 1827, the Tory party, under prime minister Lord Liverpool, was in power. These were difficult times for the government and its ministers, as the country fought wars in both Europe and North America, feared civil uprising in their own country and coped with a growing demand for parliamentary reform. The government relied on local magistrates and grandees to administer the counties and drew on local militias and parish constables to keep the peace. The two main political parties, the Whigs and Tories, were fairly closely aligned, the Whigs having more support from emerging wealthy merchants and industrialists, many of whom were

The Prince of Wales by James Gillray.

in favour of free trade, the abolition of slavery and political reform, whereas the Tories were traditionally the defenders of the status quo, landed interests and the Church of England.

At the top of all of this was King George III, who had reigned since 1760. However, he suffered from recurrent mental illness in later life, and from 1811 his eldest son George, the Prince of Wales, acted as Prince Regent, becoming King George IV on his father's death in 1820. Self-centred, lazy and profligate with both money and mistresses, the Prince Regent epitomised the very worst of human vanity, as befits the most powerful player in the world of *Vanity Fair*.

As Prince Regent and then King, George spent vast sums of money on parties, embarked on ambitious building programmes and gambled excessively. Whilst he had charm and wit, he failed to provide any kind of national leadership during the Napoleonic Wars, was deemed unreliable and irresponsible by Lord Liverpool and his ministers, and his wasteful spending during a time of war largely earned him the contempt of the people. Thackeray himself painted an unflattering portrait of him in the novel, 'florid of face, portly of person', ironically referring to him as 'Good King George'. A biography published after the King's death in 1830 concluded that George IV 'went further to the demoralization of society than any prince recorded in the pages of history'.

By 1813, Britain had been engaged in near-continual war in Europe since 1793, with war also erupting in America, although many in Britain saw this as just a minor sideshow to the conflict with France. These wars, first the Revolutionary Wars (1792–1802) and then the Napoleonic Wars (1803–15) would culminate in the Battle of Waterloo, the centrepiece of *Vanity Fair*.

'The Plumb-pudding in danger', one of James Gillray's most famous satires.

The wars involved a series of European coalitions pitted first against the French Republic and then its emperor, Napoleon Bonaparte (see page 122). From around 1797, French military successes had begun to alter the balance of power in Europe and the threat of a French invasion on British shores mounted. A brief peace between March 1802 and May 1803 was followed by war again, after which Bonaparte's Armée d'Angleterre (Army of England), 130,000 strong, amassed along the Channel coast. On high alert and expecting a French invasion on an almost hourly basis, Britain hastily constructed a vast network of coastal defences.

By October 1805, Nelson's victory over the
French and Spanish fleet at the Battle of Trafalgar
made invasion an impossibility, although in
December that year Napoleon went on to win
an important victory at Austerlitz and much of
Western Europe fell under French control. From
1810, however, Napoleon was halted in the
Iberian Peninsula by a coalition of Spain, Portugal
and Britain under the Duke of Wellington (see
page 125) and Napoleon's army was crushed when
it attacked Russia in 1812: up to half a million
of his men perished during its bitter winter. The
Battle of Leipzig, fought by a new coalition of
Prussia, Austria, Russia and Sweden in 1813 – the
largest battle Europe had ever seen, involving six
hundred thousand soldiers – resulted in a decisive
defeat for the French Empire. Napoleon was
forced to withdraw west of the Rhine, and early

ABOVE: Horatio Nelson (1758–1805).

OPPOSITE: The Battle of Trafalgar, 21 October 1805.

in 1814 a coalition of armies invaded France. On 4 April, Napoleon abdicated and was exiled to the Mediterranean island of Elba.

With the French king restored and the Treaty of Paris signed at the end of May 1814, peace celebrations erupted in Britain. The Prussian and Russian sovereigns, Austrian chancellor and various German dignitaries arrived in Britain for a grand procession in London and lavish celebrations, with the city illuminated for three nights. Feasts, balls and games were held, and church bells rang out across the country. On 1 August the Prince Regent took the opportunity to stage a Grand Jubilee, to mark the centenary of Hanoverian rule and the anniversary of the defeat of the French navy at the Battle of the Nile in 1798. History now tells us that the celebrations were premature, as the seemingly unstoppable Napoleon would return with a large army the following year. As Mr Sedley, who in the novel is made bankrupt having bought stocks in the once-buoyant French stock market, rages,

could any man ever have speculated upon the return of that Corsican scoundrel from Elba?

The Return from Elba, by C. Delort.

A vibrant and noisy city

BECKY, LIKE MANY of the characters in *Vanity Fair*, is lured by
the excitement and opportunities that await in London. Vibrant,
noisy and at times foul-smelling, London had experienced rapid
growth with newcomers arriving from across Britain and abroad.
By 1811 the capital had a population of more than a million:
a twelfth that of the country, and a hundred thousand more than
a decade before. Over the next thirty years the city's population
would double again.

MATILDA

And beware, old London town,
Miss Sharp is on her way!

The city also generated about a quarter of the country's wealth. Industrialisation and growing international trade had increased the number of traders and banks in Britain, especially in London, and by the early nineteenth century London was the trading capital of the world. In addition, thousands of small manufacturing companies – such as jewellers, carriage-makers and printers – had sprung up as demand for goods rocketed. Visitors were amazed by the variety of products on offer in London shops, unsurpassed anywhere in the world. In the 1780s a German visitor to London wrote: 'The stranger in London will be struck with astonishment when he sees the innumerable kinds of merchandize displayed before his eyes in thousands of well-fitted-up shops, for I believe there is no city in the world which in this respect can be compared to London.'

As migrants arrived, small pockets of London constantly changed in character and reputation. Covent Garden and Soho, where in the novel we learn Becky Sharp lived as a child with her artist father and French opera-girl mother, retained a dubious reputation – the preserve of immigrants (particularly Huguenot settlers from France) as well as artists, writers and entertainers. The well-to-do lived and played in Mayfair, although even here the titled dandy might have to jostle in the street with a herd of cattle on their way to slaughter. London also offered copious pleasures and entertainments, from concerts, theatres and pleasure gardens (see page 71) to taverns, gambling

YORK GATE, REGENT'S PARK, & MARY-LE-BONE CHURCH.

ABOVE: John Nash's York Gate, at the entrance to Regent's Park, with St Mary-le-Bone Church beyond.

LEFT: The house on Young Street in Kensington where Thackeray completed *Vanity Fair*.

OPPOSITE: A terrace in Russell Square.

dens (see page 110) and brothels, leading many to view the capital city as not just a place of opportunity but also one of corruption and temptation.

The appearance of London was also changing as architects set about ambitious building projects. John Nash, whose patron was George IV, was creating Regent Street and Regent's Park, with the aim to make London a distinguished and fashionable city. Regent Street, as planned by Nash in 1810, would physically separate Mayfair from Soho. The nobility were investing and building in London too. The Cavendishes – the family of the Dukes of Devonshire – were building the Burlington Arcade, a covered corridor of shops on Piccadilly. In the seventeenth and eighteenth centuries, the Russell family (the Dukes of Bedford), had developed much of Bloomsbury, the area of London where Thackeray himself lived and chose as the location for the homes of the Sedleys and the Osbornes. The large terraced houses in and around Bedford Square and Russell Square were designed for upper-middle-class families like the Sedleys, although the area could never quite shake off its bohemian air.

JOS SEDLEY

THE 'COLLECTOR OF Boggley Wollah', as he is affectionately known, is Amelia's elder brother, Jos. Twelve years Amelia's senior, he has returned from India where he works as an official for the East India Company. He is unattached and wealthy, as Becky is interested to discover – so much so that she immediately sets her sights on him, attracted more by his money and status rather than any personal allure.

Dressed in colourful silks and elaborate waistcoats, Jos cuts a dandyish, if ridiculous, figure. He loves to eat, drink and tell stories of his heroic exploits – taming rampaging elephants and the like – all of which are entirely fabricated. 'He's clearly done well out in India,' explains David Fynn, who plays Jos Sedley. 'But he probably doesn't have to exert himself too much; I'd imagine there's a lot of napping and drinking brandy on the veranda. Still, he's obviously very wealthy and often has wads of cash on him.'

David continues: 'Despite being thirty, he's quite a little boy. India allows him to take on a different role and character, but when he comes home he picks up where he left off and he hasn't quite evolved as much in his home environment.'

For that reason, when Jos is confronted by his sister's pretty friend making eyes at him, he's entirely thrown; he can't even speak, and runs away. The next day, he makes amends by buying Amelia and Becky flowers, although they make him sneeze. He is anything but a smooth operator. Becky, however, is unswayed, calms him down, and Jos is soon totally captivated by Becky and intent on proposing to her.

Things go seriously wrong, however, when he joins Amelia, George, Dobbin and Becky at the Vauxhall Pleasure Gardens. In a state of nerves, he drinks too much, causes a bit of a fight and sings in front of a crowd, and everyone is forced to leave. Nonetheless, our valiant Becky is undeterred, telling Amelia that 'as for his manners, I shall be the making of them'. The proposal, however, never happens: George convinces Jos that Becky is of too low a birth for him, and Jos leaves in humiliation.

Jos is David Fynn's first role in a television period drama. The English actor and producer's previous acting roles include Brett in the NBC series *Undateable*, as well as various National Theatre productions in London. He notes that the character of Jos is very different from his own personality: 'He really enjoys the finer things in life, and I'm not really into that. It's good to play someone who really isn't me.'

MR SEDLEY

He's as vain as a girl! He's a great deal vainer than you ever were in your life, and that's saying a good deal.

DAVID FYNN: Jos's costumes are always bright. His big thing is waistcoats. I love his coats, and they're made just a bit too snug, so he's always busting out of the seams.

In Brussels, Jos sports a magnificent moustache, along with a coat frogged like a military uniform. His aim is to look like an officer, although Rawdon tells him to cut it off as only continental soldiers have moustaches. While moustaches were a common fashion in the 1840s, when Thackeray was writing the novel, no British officer would have sported a moustache at the time of Waterloo.

David goes on to say: 'His flamboyant outfits probably compensate for the fact that he's very shy and insecure. He talks about this "other girl" to George Osborne, a girl that he met at a party ten years ago who made eyes at him. There's something really sweet about him hanging on to that. When he mucks things up with Becky, he goes back to India and probably carries that with him. That could have been his first shot at happiness, and he blew it. He's a bit of a buffoon, but he's got a heart at the same time.'

Jos next sees Becky in Brussels, where he has come because all of high society is there. As the military prepare for the Battle of Waterloo, the mood darkens; Jos, sporting a ridiculous moustache,

provides a bit of light relief in the shadow of impending war. He shows his true colours when, in the belief that Brussels is about to be overrun by the French, he takes flight, buying Becky's horses for an extortionate sum and leaving his sister behind.

After a return to India (where Jos is now the Magistrate of Bundlegunge), we next see Jos in Pumpernickel, Germany. There he comes across Becky, who is estranged from her husband Rawdon Crawley, ostracised from society and living in poverty. Becky immediately latches on to Jos, knowing that he still has a soft spot for her, and succeeds in winning him over. As a result, Jos brings Becky back into the fold, with the help of the equally over-trusting Amelia.

Thus Becky and Jos end up together, riding on the carousel that is *Vanity Fair* – although we suspect Becky may fare better than Jos, as she's the one very much in control, comfortable in the knowledge that Jos has hefty life insurance …

Boggley Wollah

JOS WORKS FOR the East India Company in what Thackeray describes as an 'honourable and lucrative position' as the official in charge of the Boggley Wollah district's taxes and revenue. In reality, the East India Company at this time was an immensely powerful private company that administrated large areas of India, monopolising commerce between India and Britain. It had a private army that was twice the size of the British army, and employed thousands of officials and traders. These officials were nominally employed to collect taxes or administer territories, but those

A portrait of Jos, dressed as an Indian nabob, seated on an elephant. Having bought the painting at the Sedley auction, Becky has the foresight to hang on to it, rolled up among her belongings, only to produce it when she sees Jos in Pumpernickel.

AMELIA

My brother, Jos.
He's the Collector of
Boggley Wollah.

AMELIA

It's in India

BECKY

What does he collect
there?

AMELIA

Do you know,
I've no idea.

BECKY

India sounds …

AMELIA

So far away!

BECKY

So exciting!

with an entrepreneurial spirit could make a lot of money, as Jos himself seems to have done.

William Thackeray was born in Calcutta, on 18 July 1811. His grandfather made a fortune trading elephants in India, which enabled him to buy a large country estate back in England. Thackeray's father, Richmond, had gone out to India in 1798, aged sixteen, and rose swiftly up the ranks of the East India Company, becoming Secretary to the Board of Revenue in 1807 and a judge at Midnapore in Bengal. Thackeray's mother Anne Becher, who married Richmond at the age of

William Thackeray with his parents.

seventeen in 1810, belonged to an English family that had lived in Bengal for several generations.

In 1815, Richmond Thackeray succumbed to fever and died, leaving a substantial inheritance of £18,000 to his son, which was to be held in trust until he was twenty-one. The following year, when he was just five years old, Thackeray was sent to school in England, arriving in 1817. His mother remained in India, later marrying her childhood sweetheart Henry Carmichael-Smyth. The young Thackeray didn't see his mother for three years – a not-uncommon practice at the time, but the separation was keenly felt by Thackeray and would be recalled decades later in his writing.

Thackeray never returned to India and it may be that his grasp on the realities of Indian life was a little limited. Jos's position as the Collector of Boggley Wollah (a fictional district) is never fully defined, as if Thackeray intentionally clouded it in obscurity, largely to enable Jos to concoct tall tales of heroic exploits in the far-flung subcontinent.

When Dobbin and Jos's regiment return to India, we learn that Jos has been promoted to Magistrate of Bundlegunge.

An English grandee of the East India Company riding in an Indian procession.

A genteel education

MISS PINKERTON'S ACADEMY for Young Ladies, where Becky and Amelia are schooled, is in Chiswick, then a genteel riverside village just outside London. It was a popular place for schools and William Thackeray himself attended a school there from 1818, from the age of seven to ten and a half. Thackeray seems to have been fairly happy at the school, and particularly so when his mother and stepfather returned from India in 1820.

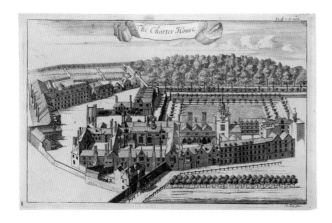

In January 1822, Thackeray moved to Charterhouse public school, then near Smithfield in London, where he was given the education 'of a gentleman'. The oppressive regime under headmaster Dr Russell, where canings were common and boys were left unsupervised outside the limited hours of teaching, had an effect on the sensitive Thackeray. In his later writings, Thackeray parodied Charterhouse as 'Slaughterhouse', and in a scene in the latter part of the novel *Vanity Fair*, little Rawdon is sent to a public school in Smithfield called Whitefriars, a thinly disguised Charterhouse. There, he suffers the same fate as his father Rawdon Crawley at Eton, and that of his creator: 'He only got that degree of beating which was, no doubt, good for him; and as for blacking shoes, toasting bread and fagging in general, were these offices not deemed to be a necessary part of every young English gentleman's education?'

Vauxhall Pleasure Gardens

VAUXHALL PLEASURE GARDENS provides a spectacular backdrop to a key scene in *Vanity Fair*, in which Jos, Becky, Amelia, George and Dobbin take in the sights, sounds and splendour of this glittering outdoor venue. Pleasure gardens were frequented by the great and the good (and not so good) throughout the eighteenth century and the first part of the nineteenth. Situated near Lambeth, Vauxhall was the biggest of its type in London and consisted of landscaped gardens, miniature waterways and shrubberies, spectacular illuminations and dedicated buildings for performances, as well as around fifty 'supper booths', which were like theatre boxes, open at the front, with a table around which six to eight people could eat.

Vauxhall was a meeting place where the wealthy could rub shoulders with members of the Royal Family, who were regular visitors, as were the middle classes. It was a place to see and to be seen, to gossip and catch up on the latest fashions. The Gardens' sizeable one-shilling-and-six admission price was intended to keep the rabble out, although well-dressed prostitutes, pickpockets and other unsavoury types were known to mingle among the crowds. In the eighteenth century, Vauxhall was an elegant and fashionable rendezvous, where the likes of George Frideric Handel performed and the painters William Hogarth and Francis Hayman displayed their work in supper booths, making the Gardens the first public art gallery in England.

By the early nineteenth century, Vauxhall was still favoured by the well-to-do, but it had evolved into a more populist commercial venue, featuring circus performers, fireworks and massed bands, where stout would be served (much to the consternation of Jos, who deems that beneath him as a gentleman). Still a feast for the senses, thousands of visitors came to drink, eat, sing, take in the lights and fireworks, grab a kiss in shady corners and enjoy a variety of acts. These ranged from gymnasts and strongmen to equestrians, and the famous tightrope walker Madame Saqui, who performed at Vauxhall from 1816. As in the series, a hermit did indeed reside in the gardens and masquerades were a popular event, such as the Grand Masquerade of 1812, which was held to celebrate successes in the Peninsular War.

Overseeing it all was the 'kind and smiling idiot' (as Thackeray described him) Mr Simpson, the famous Master of Ceremonies from 1797 to 1835. Hot-air balloons were a feature of Vauxhall, and were a great spectacle in the sky, visible across much of London and providing a real boost to the Gardens' publicity. By 1840, however, pleasure gardens were unable to compete with the advent of the music halls, and the last event at Vauxhall was held in 1859. The gardens were eaten up by the expansion of a nearby railway station, named for none other than the Battle of Waterloo.

The Sweet Lass of Richmond Hill

THE VAUXHALL PLEASURE Gardens scene in *Vanity Fair* also features a popular love ballad from the period (which is certainly familiar to Jos, who drunkenly sings along). Known as the 'Sweet Lass of Richmond Hill', it was first performed at Vauxhall in 1789. It was said to be a favourite of George III, and some mistakenly thought his son, the Prince Regent, had written it about his mistress Maria Fitzherbert. The lyrics were in fact written by Leonard McNally (1752–1820) about Frances l'Anson, whose family lived in Richmond, Yorkshire. McNally and Frances eloped, as her father disapproved of him (a nod perhaps to Becky and Amelia's own future marriage arrangements). The music was composed by James Hook (1746–1827), organist at Vauxhall Pleasure Gardens from 1774 to 1820.

On Richmond Hill there lived a lass
More bright than May-day morn,
Whose charms all other maids' surpass,
A rose without a thorn.

This lass so neat, with smile so sweet,
Has won my right good will.
I'd crowns resign to call her mine,
Sweet lass of Richmond Hill!

Ye zephyrs fair that fan the air,
And wanton through the grove,
O whisper to my charming fair,
I died for her I love.

How happy will the shepherd be
Who calls this maid his own!
O may her choice be fix'd on me!
Mine's fix'd on her alone.

CHAPTER
TWO

Miss Sharp begins to make friends

---

*You've got your feet firmly
under my table, Becky*

YOUNG BECKY HAS arrived at Sir Pitt Crawley's country estate in Hampshire. There she meets her two pupils Rose and Violet, and is further acquainted with Sir Pitt himself and his dashing officer son, Captain Rawdon Crawley. Rawdon's pious older brother, Bute, and his wife, Martha, immediately suspect Becky is a fortune-hunter and begin plotting against her. Whilst the irascible Sir Pitt rants about poachers, tenants and thieves, Becky sets about helping him with his affairs, firmly establishing herself in his esteem. Rawdon and George Osborne carouse at a gentlemen's club, only for George to be dragged away by Dobbin so that he may pay a visit to the love-sick Amelia. Queen's Crawley is set in turmoil when the moneyed Aunt Matilda Crawley arrives with Rawdon. As everyone simpers around her she utters to her nephew, 'Good God, Rawdon, are we really related to these dreadful people?' Becky charms Matilda and the ageing aunt talks to her new favourite companion as her equal. Becky dances with Sir Pitt and Rawdon falls in love with Becky. Lady Crawley is taken ill and requests that Becky looks after her. Mr Osborne suspects that Mr Sedley's fortunes are on a downturn. Becky leaves for London with a frail Matilda.

SIR PITT CRAWLEY

SIR PITT CRAWLEY, MP, makes a surprising entrance into the world of *Vanity Fair*. He is the coachman who brings Becky to the gloomy estate of Queen's Crawley – much to her astonishment when he introduces himself. However, Becky swiftly gets the measure of the man, particularly when he growls, 'I can afford as many [coachmen] as I damn well like. But I like to drive my own horses. And I don't like to teach my own children.'

Such is Sir Pitt Crawley: a country man, with a title and a huge estate, but he is gruff and rough, with a strong Hampshire accent to boot. With little concern for social niceties, in the series he's one of the few characters who is devoid of any kind of social pretension. In the novel, Becky writes in a letter to Amelia that 'Sir Pitt is not what we silly girls, when we used to read *Cecilia* at Chiswick, imagined a baronet must have been … Fancy an old, stumpy, short, vulgar, and very dirty man, in old clothes and shabby old gaiters, who smokes a horrid pipe, and cooks a horrid supper in a saucepan.'

Martin Clunes, OBE, who is certainly taller and less stumpy than the Sir Pitt of the novel, plays the part of the disreputable baronet. A much-loved star of film and television, Clunes is best known for playing Doc Martin in the ITV series of the same name. Like Sir Pitt, Clunes lives in the country, loves to work with animals, and can even drive a horse and carriage – as he did for the filming of *Vanity Fair*.

'I like playing Sir Pitt,' says Clunes, 'because he's comfortable in his own skin and space. He's slightly rubbed up the wrong way by his ghastly sons and he boasts to Becky that he's "won and lost more lawsuits than any man in England" and he is a bit of a miser. But he's almost the only person in the book who sees Becky for what she is, and appreciates her for that.'

Sir Pitt's two sons couldn't be more different from their father. His eldest is the preachy, self-satisfied Bute Crawley, who deeply disapproves of his father's godless ways. Sir Pitt admits to Becky that he only puts up with Bute and his 'prune-faced wife' Martha because he owes them money. His rakish younger son Rawdon shows little interest in the country estate and is happier with his regiment or living a life of pleasure in London.

Becky soon grasps the situation at Queen's Crawley: that Sir Pitt is drowning in lawsuits and paperwork in his attempts to deal with 'poachers, crooked agents and bankrupt tenants'. She starts to keep his papers in order and to organise the house, and Sir Pitt is immediately taken with her.

Bullied by his sister Matilda to hold a ball at Queen's Crawley, Sir Pitt has a pleasant dance with Becky, despite him warning the young governess, 'Watch your feet, mind, I haven't danced this century.' She survives the dance, but Rawdon soon whisks Becky away from his father.

THE QUEEN'S CRAWLEY BALL: The visual palette for Queen's Crawley was made of up earthy, autumnal colours. Fashions in darkest Hampshire would have been some fifteen years behind London.

RIGHT: Other than his dog, Sir Pitt is at his happiest in the company of his butler Horrocks, who is frequently inebriated.

Later in the series, the maid Betsey, daughter of Horrocks, fancies herself as the next Lady Crawley.

OPPOSITE: When Sir Pitt dies, we see his faithful dog Gorer sitting pitifully at his graveside, as if he is the only living thing that truly misses him. Clunes bonded with Gorer on set, and had in fact worked with the Irish Wolfhound before, on *Doc Martin*. As a result, Gorer appears in far more scenes that originally intended, simply because the two worked so well together.

Sir Pitt is on his second marriage, to the daughter of an ironmonger. Martin Clunes adds, 'He's not very nice about his first wife, and really not nice about his current wife. Matilda terrifies him but he needs her as she's got a lot of money. His sons are a massive disappointment to him – there's really quite a lot of dysfunction in the family. And in a period drama, that's quite unusual and rather refreshing!'

When Matilda is taken ill and insists that Becky accompany her back to London, Sir Pitt is sad to see Becky go. When his frail wife dies by falling down the stairs, he wastes no time heading off to London to get her back – 'Becky, I can't get on without you. The house all goes wrong' – and then goes down on one knee to propose: 'I'm an old man, but I'm a good 'un. I'm good for twenty year.' Of Sir Pitt, Gwyneth Hughes, the series writer, felt 'he has a real life force coursing through him, and in that way he's a good match for Becky, although of course he's too old for her and Becky turns him down.' Pitt, nonetheless, takes the rebuff in good humour and still offers his friendship, in contrast to Aunt Matilda's indignation over Becky's refusal.

Years later we see Sir Pitt older and more dishevelled, although he still has just about enough life in him to chase his young servant Betsey. The exertion, however, proves too much for him and he collapses, later dying. Rawdon is shocked by the news of his father's death, but the family's main concern is their inheritance, and it's not long before Bute and Martha sweep in to take over the estate. At Sir Pitt's funeral, it's only his servants Horrocks and Betsey who seem to truly mourn his passing, as well as his faithful dog Gorer, who poignantly guards the grave of his former master.

The ancestral home of Queen's Crawley is large, old and fairly decrepit. Sir Pitt is not an extravagant man, and one suspects that only the most essential maintenance is done. The location for Queen's Crawley was a beautiful house similarly lived in by the same family for generations, and not normally used for filming.

JULIA STANNARD: National Trust houses that are open to the public often feel too pristine and manicured. We needed something more lived-in, a setting that you can almost smell, with dogs running around. We obviously had to make a few changes for filming, but otherwise it was perfect.

BECKY

I can't bear to be a governess.
I wasn't put on his earth to be a
poor and friendless spinster.

The young governess

BECKY ARRIVES AT Queen's Crawley as a governess to Sir
Pitt's young daughters, Violet and Rose. The position of governess
was an increasingly common form of employment for women
in the nineteenth century, particularly those from middle-class
families who might have been affected by the volatile markets
and bank failures during and after the Napoleonic Wars. Living
within a household wasn't without its difficulties: governesses
were not the equal of their employers, but nor did they belong to
the servant class. They hovered somewhere in between, making
them somewhat of an outsider. Concerns also arose over having
lone, unmarried females in the house, lest they attract attention
from any gentleman in residence – so much so that advice books
recommended that employers take on plain governesses only.

Despite her initial misgivings, Becky swiftly sees that she can work
her role to her own advantage. The position enables her to have
close contact with a family much higher up the social rankings than
the Sedleys and, fortunately for her, with a master who cares little
for class distinction. She sets about making herself indispensable
to the workings of the house, largely at the expense of her two
charges, whose formal education we suspect is largely non-existent.
In the process she captivates both Sir Pitt and his rakish son
Rawdon, who, it is inferred, may have had his wicked way with the
previous governess – but who quickly realises that the indomitable
Becky is more than his match.

Old English stock

SIR PITT AND the Crawley family represent the landed aristocracy in *Vanity Fair*, 'good old English country stock', as Becky describes them, 'noble and serious, going back generations'. Through Sir Pitt, Thackeray pokes fun at the ruling classes and the whole system of social ranking. In other kinds of fiction, as Becky writes to Amelia, baronets are often depicted as handsome, elegant and generous. Instead, Sir Pitt is ageing, unrefined and penny-pinching. His lack of artifice and aristocratic sheen gives him a certain dignity – there is no pretence or façade to Sir Pitt, and unlike many in *Vanity Fair* he doesn't give a damn what anyone thinks of him.

Queen's Crawley, as described in the novel, is so named because Queen Elizabeth stopped once at Crawley for breakfast, and 'was so delighted by some remarkably fine Hampshire beer … that she forthwith erected Crawley into a borough to send two members to Parliament; and the place, from the day of that illustrious visit, took the name of Queen's Crawley'. Thackeray lists the names of Sir Pitt's ancestors, all of whom are named after people in power at the time in order to ingratiate themselves with the great and the good, as the name 'Crawley' suggests. Sir Pitt himself is named after prime minister William Pitt the elder (1708–78); his son Rawdon's namesake is Francis Rawdon-Hastings (1754–1826), a distinguished military commander in the

William Pitt the elder

ROSE

Rawdon is very
handsome, but
awfully poor on
account of being
younger than Bute.

American War of Independence and in India, and a
friend of the Prince Regent.

English society in the early 1800s was still very
much a pyramid with the aristocracy, made up
of families like the Crawleys, a small group at the
top. The difference in wealth between a nobleman
and a poor labourer at the bottom of society was
vast. The system of primogeniture, whereby eldest
sons inherited titles and lands, ensured the group
at the top remained small. Estates also were not
divided and broken up, as was common in Europe.
Younger sons might get a small amount of money
and a leg-up into a profession, such as the army,
church, politics or perhaps the East India Company
(see page 66). Tensions over inheritance often ran
high, splintering families and fostering resentment,
as is so well illustrated in *Vanity Fair* and other
novels of the period.

Land values and rent were buoyant at the start of
the nineteenth century, and during the Napoleonic
Wars landowners were able to charge more for
their crops and produce, although they, like
everyone else, complained about the new taxes
introduced to fund the war. The passing of the
Corn Laws in 1815, which placed tariffs on
imported grain and food, kept prices high and
further secured landed incomes. Many grand
families also owned property and land in the cities,
particularly in London, where land values and rents

The Bread Riot at the entrance to the House of Commons, following the passage of the infamous Corn Laws in 1815.

soared during the great Georgian building boom of the eighteenth century (see page 59). Landowners also invested in government stock, the Bank of England and trading companies, and made money from industrialisation. On their great estates, they mined materials such as slate, building stone and brick-clay, and many a great landowner promoted transport improvements such as turnpike trusts and canals. In the novel, Sir Pitt Crawley similarly speculates in every possible way, working mines, buying canal shares and breeding coach horses (although his mines flooded, and he was known to underfeed his horses).

Lord Steyne, as Master of the Powder Closet, has immense power and even the ear of the king.

An 1832 cartoon by E. King, depicting the urgent need for electoral reform.

The great landlords also maintained their pre-eminence by keeping a firm grip on political power. A significant percentage held government posts, and administered the law as magistrates and JPs. Positions at the Royal Court were particularly coveted: Lord Steyne in *Vanity Fair* is made Master of the Powder Closet, a fictitious and slightly ridiculous-sounding title, although not entirely different from the real office of Gentleman of the Bedchamber. Sir Pitt Crawley, as a baronet, is able to sit as a member of Parliament, and in the novel Thackeray describes his borough, now less populous than it once was, as 'rotten'. Prior to the parliamentary reforms of 1832, many constituencies or boroughs with virtually no population had representation in Parliament – and were known as rotten boroughs – whereas the newly emerging industrial areas with much larger populations had hardly any representation. Queen's Crawley is as rotten as they get, although Sir Pitt, in the novel, cares little for the injustice of it: 'Rotten! be hanged – it produces me a good fifteen hundred a year.'

The Reformers' Attack on the Old Rotten Tree; or, the Foul Nests of the Cormorants in Danger.

RAWDON CRAWLEY

THE YOUNG, DASHING officer who catches Becky's eye is Captain Rawdon Crawley, the younger son of Sir Pitt. Seen sitting astride a horse, Rawdon's red military uniform serves only to increase his good looks and charm, of which he's not entirely unaware.

When we first meet Rawdon he is, as Thackeray describes him in the novel, a 'perfect and celebrated "blood," or dandy about town'. A good-natured soldier, he spends much of his time with his regiment, and is fond of horses and gambling. He's good at sports and games, and frequently wins at billiards and almost any card game, often at the expense of his friends. He's not an intellectual but lives more by gut and instinct. He's also partial to the ladies: when Becky asks little Rose what happened to their last governess, she answers matter-of-factly 'Rawdon …' – leaving us only to imagine what happened.

Captain Crawley does come home to Queen's Crawley, but largely to ask Sir Pitt for a hand-out – it's clear he's not much of a country man like his father. Tom Bateman, the actor playing Rawdon, says, 'His view of the family is that they're a bunch of country bumpkins and quite boring. His relationship with his dad is not all bad, but I wouldn't say they're best friends.'

The British actor, best known for his roles in the television series *Jekyll & Hyde* and *Da Vinci's Demons*, and the film *Murder on the Orient Express*, is a real fan of the novel and has read it quite a

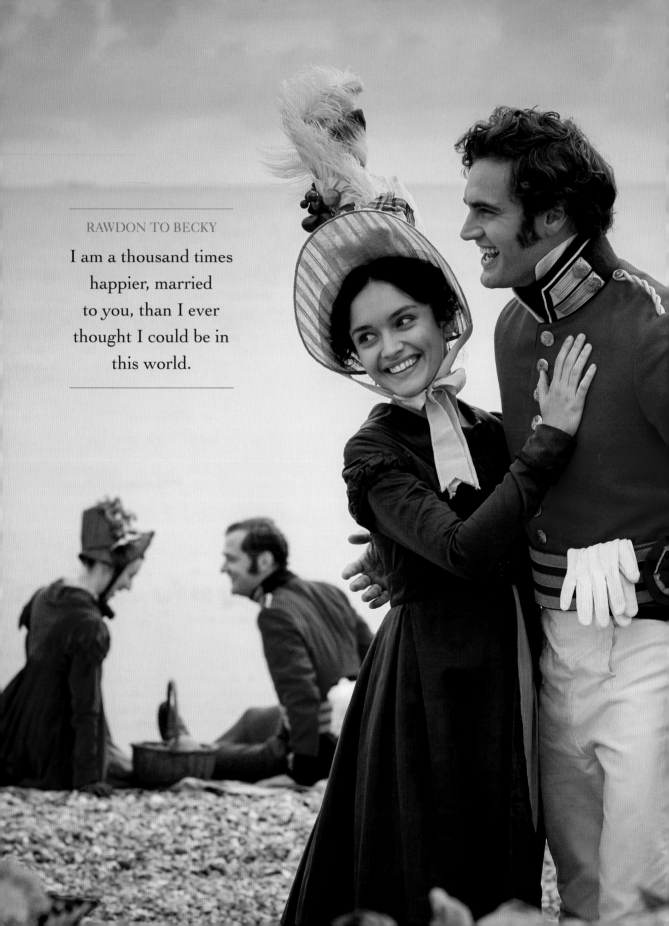

RAWDON TO BECKY

I am a thousand times
happier, married
to you, than I ever
thought I could be in
this world.

few times. 'What I like about Thackeray is that he writes about people, their souls, heart and conscience. The book feels modern, because even if the world and language is different, there are common themes and issues that are relevant today. For me, *Vanity Fair* explores the lengths people are willing to go to to secure what they think is happiness.'

'Becky is of course at the epicentre of *Vanity Fair*, and Rawdon falls in love with her,' Tom adds. 'At first he thinks of her as just another pretty governess that he can win over, but very quickly he sees that she is a match for him. He keeps trying to flirt with her, and all of the lines that usually work with others just don't work with Becky – she gets the better of him. And, of course, you want what you can't have; when she rebuffs him, that gets his interest going.'

Another key person in Rawdon's life is his aunt, Matilda Crawley. The only member of the family the disapproving aunt seems to like is Rawdon, and as a result there's an understanding that he'll inherit a large legacy when she dies. Rawdon is of course mindful of this, as is Becky, and together they do everything they can to keep in the old lady's good books. What they don't foresee, however, is that Aunt Matilda is horrified by their secret marriage, having previously claimed that she was all for equality and for women marrying above their station. 'To Rawdon? Married?' she exclaims on learning about the elopement. 'Monster!

Wretch! Traitor!' The couple hope that Aunt Matilda's indignation
will soften when she hears of Rawdon's heroics on the battlefield at
Waterloo, but she is unwavering and eventually cuts Rawdon (by
now Colonel Crawley) out of her will.

Thereon, with little money to their name, Becky and Rawdon
are forced to live off credit, Rawdon's gambling wins and Becky's
schemes to keep their heads above water. Things continue to
unravel when they have a child; it's clear that Becky has little
instinct for mothering and is unable to show the love that their

son needs. Rawdon, on the other hand, is besotted with little Rawdy and this causes further tension in the marriage. As the story progresses, Rawdon changes, maturing into an older, wiser and more sympathetic person, and he can see that Becky is never satisfied. 'The audience goes on that journey with Rawdon,' says Tom, 'and Thackeray uses the character of Rawdon to highlight the fickle shallowness of everything Becky and the rest of society are hunting for. Unlike Rawdon, Becky doesn't really change, and that's her downfall.'

Becky is determined to reach the upper echelons of society and embarks on a dangerous liaison with Lord Steyne, who showers her with money and gifts. After Becky fails to bail Rawdon out when he is sent to the debtors' prison, and he then catches her with Steyne, he decides enough is enough. He attacks Steyne, violently throws him out of the house and rips Becky's diamonds off her,

their marriage well and truly shattered. To avoid further violence or even a duel, Lord Steyne arranges for Rawdon to be made Governor-General of Coventry Island, a far-flung outpost off the Ivory Coast, where Rawdon eventually succumbs to yellow fever. It's a wretched ending for Rawdon, as the series writer Gwyneth Hughes, who has a particular fondness for the character, sums up: 'He's a man felled by the love of the wrong woman, and the conclusion of his story is really sad.'

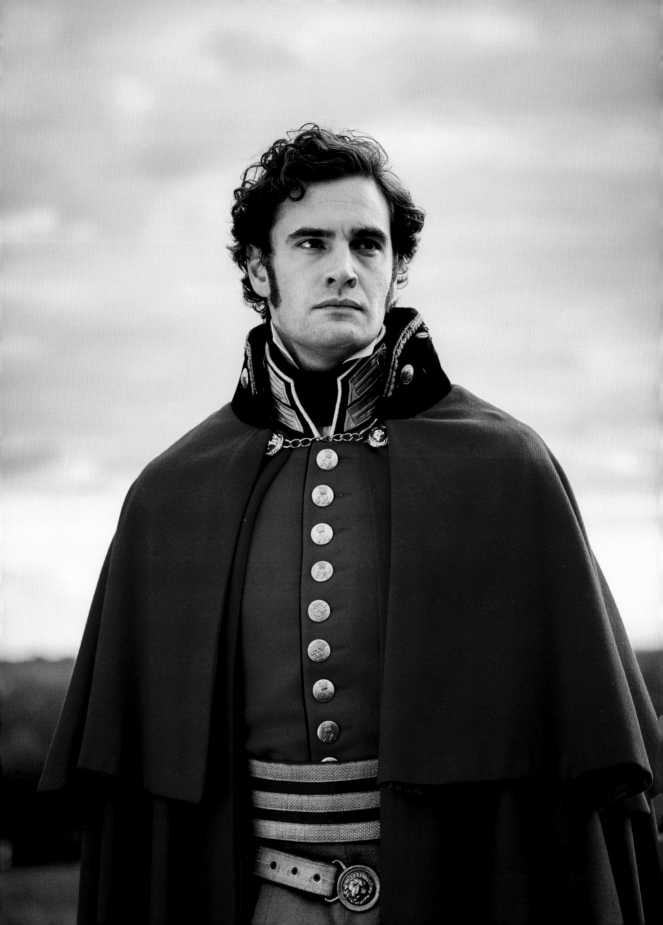

Gentlemen's pursuits

RAWDON CRAWLEY, THE quintessential man-about-town in *Vanity Fair*, is a lover of sports and the gambling tables, and a frequenter of the many clubs in London that facilitated these kinds of gentlemanly pursuits. In certain parts of Regency London, the sight of exquisitely dressed young men gambling, drinking and behaving badly was a common one – so much so that they became a recognised social figure known as the dandy.

The Prince Regent

These men with money to burn were products of prosperity, born from their families' estates or facilitated by credit issued by banks and money-lenders. In 1814, London was also flooded with army officers released from military duties abroad and keen to meet young women or gamble away their money. The top dog among the fast and fashionable set was, of course, the Prince Regent, who gambled huge sums, liked to keep up with fashions and frequented the various clubs that clamoured for his patronage.

BECKY

Cards, billiards, the roulette table. Lord knows what they see in any of it. I think of it as a useful way of keeping all foolish gentlemen out of trouble.

In *Vanity Fair*, Rawdon, George and Dobbin, and other men like them, are often found at gentlemen's clubs, places they can escape to, away from the more female, domestic arena of the home. In the novel, Matilda Crawley tells Becky that Rawdon is 'adored in his regiment; and all the young men at Wattier's [*sic*] and the Cocoa-Tree swear by him'. Rawdon also mentions he's played billiards at the Cocoa-Tree, winning £200 off George, and frequents the Regent Club on St James's Street in Mayfair. Later in the series, Becky and Rawdon set up a gaming room in their rented London house, where Becky tells Rawdon he 'will win, except when I judge it helpful for you to lose'.

The pre-eminent dandy and arbiter of fashion, Beau Brummell.

The club Watier's, in Piccadilly, was established in 1807 and named after the Prince of Wales's chef, Jean-Baptiste Watier. The most famous dandy in the land, Beau Brummell, joined and became its perpetual president, and soon the club's chief entertainment was gambling. The usual card game was Macao, a form of vingt-et-un, and eye-watering sums could be won or lost in a night. Scrope Berdmore Davies, the son of a vicar and a friend of Lord Byron, seemed to have lived purely by gambling. He won and lost thousands at Watier's: he was worth £22,000 in 1815, but just £5000 the following year.

St James's was the location of a number of well-known gentlemen's clubs, including White's, Brooks's and Boodle's, all of which still exist today. Many of these clubs had their origins in the old coffee houses that had proliferated in the seventeenth and eighteenth centuries, and were often associated with political factions. White's and the Cocoa-Tree in Pall Mall, both Tory haunts, had first been chocolate houses, when chocolate-drinking had been all the rage for the well-heeled in the eighteenth century. Both clubs were known for gambling – Hell was depicted as the inner gaming room at White's in the sixth painting of William Hogarth's *Rake's Progress*, showing Tom Rakewell having just gambled away his fortune amid a scene of chaos, where no one notices that the building is on fire. It was at White's that George Harley Drummond, of the banking family, lost £20,000 in a game of whist with Beau Brummell. At the Cocoa-Tree in 1780, the equivalent of £180,000 in today's money was bet on the roll of a single die.

Almack's in King Street, just off St James's Square, was the most exclusive of all the clubs, although it was known for its assembly rooms and balls rather than gaming. It famously turned away the Duke of Wellington twice, once for being late and another time for wearing trousers rather than breeches.

Slaughter's, the famous coffee house in Covent Garden, crops up a number of times in the novel *Vanity Fair* – Dobbin stays there, his 'old haunt', on his return to England: 'Long years had passed since he saw it last, since he and George, as young men, had enjoyed many a feast, and held many a revel there.' Coffee houses were another venue where men could meet, talk, conduct their business, send and receive mail, and learn of news relevant to their affairs, such as stock prices and the like. Slaughter's had long been popular with the artistic, and a huge number of well-known painters were known to frequent it, including William Hogarth and Thomas Gainsborough. William Thackeray was a visitor and stayed there with his stepfather in 1829.

MIDNIGHT. *Tom & Jerry at a Coffee Shop near the Olympic.*

Gambling and club life

WILLIAM THACKERAY WAS no stranger to the gaming tables. After his schooling at Charterhouse, he went up to Trinity College, Cambridge in 1828. His studies, however, suffered as he preferred to spend his time at wine parties and soon fell into the fast gambling set. In May 1830 he found himself £1500 in debt after playing at écarté with a group of professional card-hustlers. As an undergraduate, he also spent time in Paris, where he visited the great gaming house, Frascati's: in a letter Thackeray admitted that he was strongly captivated by the spectacle of the place, and it was only when 'I lost my piece' that he was able to tear himself away. Even then, he could think of nothing else for the new few days. His gambling and trips away resulted him leaving Cambridge without a degree in June 1830.

After a mini grand tour in Europe, Thackeray became a pupil at Middle Temple in London in 1831. The attractions of the capital – its taverns, gaming houses, brothels and theatres (of which Thackeray was a regular visitor) – again proved too much of a lure and his law studies suffered. Thackeray was far from being an aristocratic playboy – his father had been a middle-class civil servant in India – but he was on the fringes of the fashionable world and knew some of its people, and his sneaking fondness for this milieu would surface in *Vanity Fair* and his later writings. With mounting debts, Thackeray abandoned the law in 1833 and became increasingly interested in contemporary journalism, expressing an interest to buy or found a periodical of his own.

In 1832, Thackeray had turned twenty-one and finally came into his £18,000 inheritance, and in 1833 invested in a weekly newspaper, the *National Standard*, which he took over as editor

and proprietor. By November that year, however, all of his money had gone, much of it soaked up by the collapse of two Indian banking houses and his gambling debts. The *National Standard* soon went under, and in 1834 he was back in Paris, now with the intention to study as an artist. As his finances tightened, however, he began to work for a handful of periodicals, including *Fraser's Magazine*, the *Morning Chronicle* and *Punch*. In 1835, he met the seventeen-year-old Isabella Shawe, and married her the following year.

After a brief spell in Paris, they returned to London. Thackeray continued to work as a journalist, publishing articles and fiction either anonymously or under a number of comic pseudonyms. 'The Yellowplush Papers' (1837–8), 'A Shabby Genteel Story' (1840) and 'Barry Lyndon' (1844) all appeared in *Fraser's*, and 'The Book of Snobs' (1846–7) in *Punch*. He also produced a range of travel writing, including *The Paris Sketch Book* in 1840, which provided much-needed income.

Thackeray undertook much of his writing in London clubs, including the Garrick Club, which had opened in 1831 and Thackeray had joined two years later. The Garrick was a place where 'actors and men of refinement could meet on equal terms', at a time when actors were not generally considered respectable; the club was named after the eighteenth-century actor David Garrick. Charles Dickens was also a member, and while Thackeray and Dickens were professional rivals, they circulated within the same social circles.

DINING-ROOM OF THE GARRICK CLUB.

Thackeray and Dickens at the time of their quarrel.

In 1858, however, a scandal that became known as the Garrick Club Affair would damage their relationship. In that year, Dickens had separated from his wife, Kate, and was concerned about how his affair with the actress Ellen Ternan would be received in public. Discovering that Thackeray had been telling other people about the liaison, Dickens sanctioned the publication of an article by a young journalist, Edmund Yates, in *Household Words*, the weekly magazine Dickens edited. In it, Yates attacked Thackeray's appearance and writing: 'Mr Thackeray is forty-six years old, though, from the silvery whiteness of his hair, he appears somewhat older … His bearing is cold and uninviting, his style of conversation either openly cynical or affectedly good-natured and benevolent; his *bonhomie* is forced … Our own opinion, that his success is on the wane. His writings were never understood or appreciated even by the middle classes … there is a want of heart in all he writes.' Thackeray was not upset so much by the attack, but that Yates had written about conversations that had taken place at the Garrick Club. It was thought bad form to report on what went on inside the club – gentlemen's clubs were private places with a code of secrecy, which he felt Yates had violated. In the end, Yates's membership to the club was cancelled, but Thackeray and Dickens's amicable relationship would never recover.

AUNT MATILDA

THE FORMIDABLE AUNT Matilda, played by British actress Frances de la Tour, is Sir Pitt Crawley's sister. Her immense wealth turns everyone around her into simpering wretches, all of them keen to get their hands on her money once she has died. She, as a result, finds the whole family particularly repellent, so much so that they when she turns up unexpectedly at Queen's Crawley she remarks to her nephew, 'Good God, Rawdon, are we really related to these dreadful people?'

Unlike the rest of the family, Matilda has always doted on Rawdon, his devil-may-care charm appealing to her. Once Becky learns from Violet that Matilda is 'the richest lady in the whole wide world', she immediately sets on a scheme 'to make Aunt Matilda fall at our feet'. The plan works, so much so that when Matilda is taken ill she asks for Becky to return to London with her, much to the indignation of Matilda's long-suffering servant Briggs.

In summing up Becky, Matilda claims to be a radical, and a believer in social equality: 'If merit has its just reward, Miss Sharp ought to sit where you do. Ought indeed to be a duchess ... I consider that particular young lady to be my equal in every respect.' In fact, Matilda is nothing other

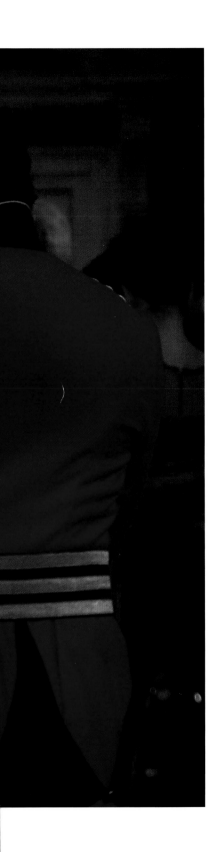

than a snob, turning her nose up at the 'middling sort' of the Sedleys and baulking when they invite her in to their house 'without a proper invitation'. When she discovers that Rawdon has secretly married Becky, she's appalled and almost sickened by the match, now describing Becky as a 'treasure hunter! Revolutionary!'

As a result, unmoved by Becky and Rawdon's attempts to repair the relationship, Matilda rewrites her will and remains steadfast in her resolve to exclude her nephew, despite his heroics at Waterloo. On their return to Brussels, Becky and Rawdon discover Matilda has had a stroke, and she dies unable to speak or rail against Becky as she sits at her bedside in London.

Matilda's final revenge is to leave Rawdon with the worthless battle relics that Becky had sent her – a serious misjudgement on Becky's part – and just £20 'in full valuation of my esteem for the choices he has made in his life'.

MATILDA

Death will come for me and I shall face him alone, for I have done no good in my life. None. I will be one of those pathetic women who die unmourned.

CHAPTER

THREE

A quarrel about an heiress

I could be good.
I could be very good on five
thousand a year

BECKY IS NOW Aunt Matilda's favourite companion. We learn that Napoleon has escaped and the Duke of Wellington is gathering his forces. Back in Hampshire, Sir Pitt Crawley is gloomy, unable to cope without Becky. When Lady Crawley falls down the stairs and dies, Sit Pitt heads straight to London and pleads with Becky to come back to his house as his wife. Becky turns him down and we discover she has secretly married Rawdon. Matilda is appalled to discover Becky's secret. The Sedleys are bankrupt, Mr Osborne calls in his debts, and they are forced to sell the house and its contents. At the auction, Dobbin bids for and wins Amelia's piano. Mr Sedley commands Amelia to break off the engagement with George Osborne, and she writes to him. Rawdon, George and Dobbin are given their marching orders. Becky writes to Matilda pleading reconciliation before Rawdon goes off to war. Mr Sedley suggests George should marry Miss Swartz, but George refuses. Rawdon and Becky try to reconcile with Matilda – she tells them to go to the lawyers the next morning, where they learn Rawdon is bestowed a measly £20. In defiance of their parents' wishes, Amelia and George marry. As war clouds gather, our band of elopers set course for Belgium.

Napoleon on the deck of the *Bellerophon* before being exiled to St Helena.

Napoleon Bonaparte

Napoleon Bonaparte (1769–1821), Emperor of the French and one of the greatest military leaders in history, had in April 1814 been exiled to the isle of Elba, off the west coast of Italy. The news that 'Boney' had escaped in the February of the following year and landed at Cannes on 1 March with fifteen hundred men sent shockwaves around Europe. The restored Louis XVIII fled to Ghent on 12 March and Napoleon triumphantly entered Paris a week later. By 25 March 1815, Austria, Prussia, Britain and Russia had concluded an alliance against Napoleon, and the British troops, among them our fictional heroes Captain Dobbin, Captain Osborne and Captain Crawley, were to prepare for their marching orders.

PAPERBOY

Boney on the loose! Our old enemy gathering his forces! Wellington recalled to command!

Throughout the Napoleonic Wars, the figure of Napoleon, scourge of Europe and 'Corsican upstart', had dominated the British imagination, particularly during the very real invasion scares of 1798 and 1803. Artists of the day, such as James Gillray and George Cruikshank, depicted Napoleon as a terrifying dwarfish figure (in fact, at 5 feet 6 inches, he was of average height) capable of committing hideous atrocities. Mothers would warn their children that if they didn't behave 'Boney' would come. However, not everyone in Britain viewed Napoleon as an evil tyrant: to some, particularly in the north, he was a working man's hero; in high society he went in and out of fashion (in the novel *Vanity Fair*, various characters, particularly Whig supporters, hold Napoleon in high esteem); and teenage girls were even attracted to the dashing and dangerous military commander. Napoleon's brief return to power in 1815 was no less admirable, many preferring him to the 'Popish rabble' then tyrannising France. Those of a romantic persuasion were particularly effusive: Lord Byron wrote in 1815 that 'It is impossible not to be dazzled and overwhelmed by his character and career.'

After Waterloo, thousands flocked to see his travelling carriage, which had been captured during the battle, when it was exhibited in London in 1816; Napoleon busts graced the mantelpieces of great houses up and down the country; and after his death in 1821, in exile on St Helena, people collected memorabilia of all kinds – from teaspoons to his bicorne hat, a tooth and even, some say, his penis, cut off during his autopsy, as well as his death mask and his last cup.

The Duke of Wellington

Born in Dublin in 1769 to an aristocratic Anglo-Irish family, the Honourable Arthur Wellesley joined the British army at the age of eighteen. He saw action in India from 1796 to 1805 and soon proved himself an able soldier and diplomat. He rose to prominence as commander of the British forces during the Peninsular campaign of the Napoleonic Wars, successfully driving French forces out of Portugal and Spain. He was made Viscount Wellington in 1809, and then granted a dukedom in 1814.

After Napoleon's exile on Elba, Wellington was appointed Britain's ambassador to the restored king of France and in February 1815 attended the Congress of Vienna, an assembly made up of the great powers of Europe who had been instrumental in overthrowing Napoleon. Before they had concluded a treaty, news came through of Napoleon's escape and Wellington was forced to leave Vienna and assemble troops in Brussels. His victory at Waterloo, alongside that of the Prussian army under Gebhard Leberecht von Blücher, and the defeat of Napoleon, would ultimately lead to the Iron Duke being revered as Britain's great military hero – 'the last great Englishman', as the poet Alfred, Lord Tennyson hailed him.

From 1828 to 1830 and briefly in 1834 Wellington served controversially as prime minister, and he continued as one of the leading Tory figures in the House of Lords until his retirement from politics in 1846. Wellington died, aged eighty-three, at Walmer Castle in Kent on 14 September 1852. He was given a state funeral, and interred next to Lord Nelson in St Paul's Cathedral.

AMELIA SEDLEY

… she had a pair of eyes which sparkled with the brightest and honestest good-humour, except indeed when they filled with tears, and that was a great deal too often; for the silly thing would cry over a dead canary-bird; or over a mouse, that the cat haply had seized upon …

AMELIA SEDLEY'S FORTUNES take a turn for the worse when her father's business collapses: the family lose their fine house and she is forced to break off her engagement with her childhood sweetheart.

Up until that point, Amelia has lived a comfortable life, within a loving and well-to-do family and secure in the knowledge that she will marry family friend George Osborne. George and Amelia's fathers are friends and business associates (Mr Sedley a stockbroker and Mr Osborne a banker) and the engagement works in everyone's favour. As Claudia Jessie, who plays Amelia, explains: 'The arrangement makes Amelia very happy – to her, George is the most perfect and handsome man ever, and he's the love of her life.'

Of Amelia's character, Claudia says: 'Amelia is soft and sweet, the kind of person who would, as Thackeray puts it, "cry over a dead canary-bird"! She has a big heart but she's also incredibly resilient, which is a quality that often you only realise you have when bad things happen. Amelia goes through a lot but keeps moving forward; she never gives up hope.'

CLAUDIA JESSIE: They made my hair lighter and more ginger, as I have dark-brown hair. They wanted a contrast between me and Becky. Make-up wise, they wouldn't have had mascara or eyeliner; it's all fairly natural and subtle.

LEFT: Amelia with George's sister Jane.

Claudia, whose previous television roles include the BBC series *WPC 56* and *Line of Duty*, has hugely enjoyed getting to grips with the story of *Vanity Fair*, its satirical take on people's hunger to achieve and its honest portrayal of people, their failings, their brilliance and how 'it's okay to be unremarkable', says Claudia.

'Like Amelia,' continues Claudia, 'I'm quite an emotional person, so I can relate to her in that way. Sometimes I probably "feel" a bit too much, which I suppose is useful when you're an actress! But I don't think I'm quite as stubborn or steadfast as Amelia.'

A central strand in the story of *Vanity Fair* is the friendship of Amelia and Becky. They meet at Miss Pinkerton's and the contrast between the two is stark: Amelia has had a sheltered, cushioned life, and she is girlish and naïve. Becky has had a more difficult, lowly upbringing and has been forced to grow up – ever since she was eight years old, as she claims later in the series.

'Amelia and Becky are from different worlds and are intrigued by each other,' explains Claudia. 'Amelia also sees this young woman with no family in need, and I think really feels for Becky at first. She wants simply to help Becky and I think she admires her courage in speaking up for herself.'

Becky in turn latches on to Amelia, partly because of the opportunity the friendship provides: she's able to stay with Amelia's family in London, and soon sets her sights on Amelia's wealthy and unattached brother, Jos. Amelia is really excited by the prospect of Becky and Jos getting together, because she and Becky will be 'happy wives and sisters for ever'. 'Becky finds Amelia pathetically adorable at first,' says Claudia, 'and is a little entertained by the fact that she seems to cry about everything, but I think her respect for Amelia grows as the story progresses, and then of course they have a big fall-out.'

GWYNETH HUGHES: Amelia and George head off to Brussels just after they get married. It's not much of a honeymoon, is it!

The fall-out occurs on the eve of Waterloo, when in a dramatic scene Amelia confronts Becky about her overt flirtation with George, who is now her husband. In defiance of their respective fathers, Amelia and George have secretly married, leading Mr Osborne to cut off all ties with his son, both personally and financially. The couple are now in Brussels with Becky, Rawdon and Dobbin, awaiting the impending battle along with the rest of the British troops. Tensions runs high and George's increasing obsession with Becky, obvious to all and encouraged by Becky, proves too much for Amelia: 'For shame, Rebecca. Bad and wicked woman. False friend and false wife,' she rails. 'Leave me. I cannot bear the sight of you.'

'George sees this powerful woman who is clearly on the up,' says Claudia, 'and he can see his life with Amelia is on a downturn. Amelia fades away from him. The power of Becky shines brighter. When money and security are swept away from the couple, Amelia is fine; she's not overly concerned about social status, she just wants to be with George and she is very much driven by love.'

She thought about him the very first moment on waking; and his was the very last name mentioned in her prayers. She never had seen a man so beautiful or so clever: such a figure on horseback: such a dancer: such a hero in general.

CLAUDIA JESSIE: The palette for my clothes and make-up changed in the series. I'm in bright pinks and greens, quite sweet colours, at the start, then I start to fade away a bit in lighter colours, and then when people start to die around me and I'm in mourning I'm in a lot of black!

'But for George, that is not enough,' Claudia continues, 'and that's when we start to see holes in their relationship. He does adore her – there nothing not to adore as Amelia is so sweet. Sadly, the moment he realises that is just before he goes away to war, which is of course too late.'

On learning of George's death on the battlefield, Amelia is inconsolable and barely able to function in her grief. The birth of their son Georgy, who is the image of his father, is what saves Amelia. As described by Thackeray, he was 'Amelia's heart and treasure … she tended the boy … with a constant passion of love'. Amelia embodies the Victorian ideal of a virtuous mother figure, in stark contrast to Becky, who is unable to show motherly love or even much interest in her own child. Later, Amelia is forced to give up the care of Georgy to the Osbornes, which causes her particular anguish.

Throughout all of Amelia's tribulations, Dobbin remains a friend to both her and his childhood friend George. As soon as Dobbin sees Amelia after she leaves school, he is hopelessly in love. The steadfast friend that he is, though, prevents him from doing anything about it because he must honour George and Amelia's engagement. Instead, he channels that love into supporting and protecting Amelia, cajoling George to look after and then marry her, writing to her, sending her money and letting her know that she's not alone when she's left a widow after Waterloo.

While we can see that Dobbin is truly worthy of her love, Amelia can't let go of George and retains an unflagging attachment to his memory and to what she thought her life would be. This blind worship of her dead husband, a man who had just before his death planned to run away with Becky, exposes Amelia's weakness, particularly as it's increasingly obvious that Dobbin worships her.

CLAUDIA JESSIE: There is so much love in *Vanity Fair.* There is of course Amelia's love for George, the love between Becky and Amelia, Dobbin's love for Amelia, Rawdon's love of Becky, there's love in the Sedley family and tons of love between Amelia and her son – I could go on!

As Claudia says, 'For Amelia, the thought of being with Dobbin feels like a betrayal, a sign that she's let go of George and the life planned for her. Everyone wants to shout, "Come on, Amelia, open your eyes!" – which Becky does in the end, because she's so furious with her!' Amelia's eyes are finally opened when Dobbin returns to Pumpernickel and declares his love for her. She finally allows herself to move on and marry Dobbin, although Dobbin realises that he too has been deluded, that Amelia is not the woman he thought she was. Amelia recognises and accepts this; as a husband, he is still as gentle and kind as ever, but the love of his life is now their daughter Janey.

Of all the characters in *Vanity Fair*, Amelia goes on one of the most interesting journeys. Series writer Gwyneth Hughes says: 'It would be easy to think of Amelia as feeble and a bit of a wuss, someone who cries all the time, but in fact she's incredibly proud and almost the Victorian ideal of a strong-willed maternal figure. Amelia changes in a way that Becky doesn't. Amelia starts as a little girl and grows into a woman. It's very moving.'

Claudia agrees: 'Amelia has such a huge journey – from being young and free, then panicked, distraught and desperately unhappy. She's really pushed to the limits and it's beautiful to see someone having to live in a quietly noble way.'

Merchant men

MR SEDLEY

Is the honour of our family completely worthless to you? That man has made us bankrupt! Our name can never be united with that of Osborne. Never. Never.

THE SEDLEYS AND Osbornes are prosperous families who live comfortable lives in fine London houses. Their wealth is not born from centuries of land-ownership but is 'new money' from trade and banking: Mr Sedley is a stockbroker and Mr Osborne a banker. Their rise in fortune and wealth has been swift – Mr Osborne's father was a butcher – but just as they have risen up the social ladder rapidly, they can lose everything with just as much speed.

MR OSBORNE

I'm a self-made man but I raised my son a gentleman. And he repays me by marrying in the gutter.

Mr Sedley's bankruptcy has catastrophic effects for the whole family; not only do they lose their house and status, but Amelia is also forced to cut off her engagement with George Osborne. There is nothing but bitterness and hostility between the two former friends, Mr Sedley and Mr Osborne. Unable to repay Osborne the debt he is now demanding, Sedley blames the other man for his downfall and Mr Osborne has little pity for his old friend. Tensions over the affair remain high and Mr Osborne refuses to accept the marriage of George to Amelia, and dramatically disowns him. In *Vanity Fair*, families, friends and lovers are torn apart by concerns over money and social status, and cruel ambition and conceitedness stalk every walk of life.

New money

THE MERCHANT CLASSES had grown in number during the eighteenth and early nineteenth centuries as a result of growing international trade, an increase in manufacturing and technological innovations, and the rapid growth of banks in London and across the country. The government, still in debt from the American War of Independence (1775–83), was forced to increase taxes to fund the wars against the French, introducing the first income tax in 1799, and to raise huge loans, which the bankers and brokers provided.

The immense strain of financing the wars included funding costly fortifications along the southern coast of England in order to repel a French invasion. For many working people, increased taxes and high food prices caused real hardship and social unrest, and Napoleon's Continental System of 1806–14, in which France blocked trade with Britain, saw shares and stocks plummet. Despite the difficulties, industry and trade survived the wars and the country had better transport links, with improved roads, bridges, a network of canals, and a fast-approaching railway age. Those with land benefited from the increase in food and agricultural prices, and some canny merchants, manufacturers and bankers grew rich from the wars. But the markets were volatile and an increasing number of smaller banks failed: many investors – like Mr Sedley, who in the novel had invested in French stocks when they were buoyant in 1814 – would lose their fortunes. The shake-up resulted in a rationalisation of the banking system, with larger, more prosperous banks, such as those of Rothschild and Baring, surviving and dominating world banking.

ABOVE: The London Stock Exchange.

BELOW: The German banker Nathan Mayer Rothschild.

A View from the Royal Exchange.

As the wars ended, the rate and scale of bankruptcies peaked. Continuing high prices, aided by the implementation of the Corn Laws in 1815, low wages and high unemployment as three hundred thousand soldiers and sailors returned from the wars contributed to a rumbling of discontent that would manifest as political unrest. This febrile economy in the years after Waterloo was also compounded by a volcanic eruption far away in Indonesia, which led to abnormal weather, low temperatures, failed harvests and famine, particularly in 1816, which was known as the 'year with no summer'.

The value of money

THE THEME OF money is a constant driving force in *Vanity Fair*.
Becky is on the hunt to secure more of it (and social status in the
process), rakish young men gamble vast sums of it, banks collapse
and debt causes ruin. We learn that Rawdon is left just £20, and
later £100, by his aunt Matilda Crawley; on the eve of battle at
Waterloo, Becky estimates her current worth as £600 to £700;
and according to Mr Osborne, Miss Swartz is worth a whopping
£200,000. But in the world of *Vanity Fair*, what do these sums
actually mean, and how do they translate in today's money?

Ours is a ready-money society. We live among bankers and City big-wigs, and be hanged to them, and to every man, as he talks to you, is jingling his guineas in his pocket.

Money was broken down in to pennies, shillings, pounds and guineas. There were 12 pence in a shilling, 20 shillings in a pound and 21 shillings in a guinea.

A penny could buy you a hot-cross bun or two, or the lyrics of two songs to sing.

A working-class labourer or street-seller would expect to earn between 7 and 15 shillings a week. That would be enough to pay for an individual's rent, food, fuel and repairs to clothing, but not enough to feed a family.

A night at the theatre could cost between a shilling and a guinea, depending on the venue and the seat. Entrance to Vauxhall Pleasure Gardens was one [shilling] and six [pence], but doubled to three shillings on special occasions.

£50 a year would be sufficient for a widow, such as that of a minor tradesman, with few outgoings.

£50 to £100 a year was a good wage for someone like a governess or butler, who would also be given bed and board. Many luxury goods, like horses or paintings, would cost this much per item.

£2500 to £5000 would be enough to build a country mansion.

MISS SWARTZ

Love may be felt for any young lady endowed with such qualities as Miss Swartz possessed; and a great dream of ambition entered into old Mr Osborne's soul, which she was to realize.

MR OSBORNE, HAVING insisted that his son cut off all ties with Amelia, wastes no time in promoting other matches for George. Top of his list are ladies with money, and Amelia's former schoolfriend Miss Swartz fits the bill perfectly. An heiress from the West Indies, Rhoda Swartz is immensely wealthy, to the tune of 'two hundred thousand pounds. Diamonds as big as pigeons' eggs,' as Mr Osborne puts it. The colour of her skin – which in this period could well have excluded Miss Swartz from high society – is of no concern to Mr Osborne; it's her money he's after.

The Caribbean was important to Britain, largely because of the huge fortunes that could be made from the trade of sugar, a prized commodity during the eighteenth century. In the novel, Miss Swartz's late father is said to have been a German-Jewish slave-owner, and she owns plantations, probably also worked by slaves. Many in Britain had profited vastly from the expansion of empire into the Americas and West Indies, and the forced transportation of millions of enslaved Africans across the Atlantic. By 1807, however, and thanks to such abolitionist campaigners as William Wilberforce, the sale and purchase of slaves was made illegal in Britain, and slavery was abolished throughout the British

Empire in 1833. Many in Britain viewed slavery as barbaric, although abolitionists faced violent opposition, not least from the slave-traders of Bristol and Liverpool.

We meet Sam, the Sedleys' servant, early on in the series, and he proves to be a sharp and enterprising individual who sees Becky for what she is. The Sedleys are entirely comfortable with having a black servant in the house, while Aunt Matilda is clearly shocked by his presence. When the Sedleys are forced to sell up, we learn that Sam is to set himself up as the owner of a public house. In the early nineteenth century, black people were not an unusual sight, particularly in London and in the former slave-trading ports of Bristol and Liverpool: it has been estimated that up to 3 per cent of Londoners at the time were black. Those who came to Britain were often brought by plantation owners and workers, government officials and military and naval officers, and many worked as butlers or other household attendants in great houses. An American visitor in 1805 was quite surprised and impressed by the presence of non-slaves in Britain: 'A black footman is considered a great acquisition and consequently negro servants are sought for and caressed. An ill-dressed or starving negro is never seen in England and in some instances even alliances are formed between them and white girls of the lower orders of society.'

Wedding matters

Both Becky and Amelia marry, in weddings that are secret and hurried. In fact, most weddings during the Georgian period were small, understated affairs, often attended by only close relatives.

Weddings were performed in church after the reading of banns and usually held before lunchtime, hence the 'wedding breakfast'. Some brides wore white – when Jane Austen's niece Anna married in 1814 she wore 'a dress of fine white muslin' – but many brides simply wore their Sunday best. Veils became popular later in the century; most brides as this time wore flowers in their hair, a cap or even a hat. The ceremony – in which the couple say 'I will', not 'I do' in accordance with the 1662 *Book of Common Prayer* – involved the giving of a ring from groom to bride, but neither the husband nor wife was obliged to wear a wedding ring, and it was highly unusual for men to do so.

CHAPTER

FOUR

In which Becky joins her regiment

Mrs Crawley, you look ravishing. All eyes are on you tonight

OUR OFFICERS AND camp followers prepare to leave for Brussels. Dobbin talks to Mr Osborne but he refuses to forgive George for marrying Amelia Sedley, scores out George's name from the family bible and burns his last will and testament. In Brussels, George and Amelia come across Major and Mrs O'Dowd, and mingle with people of quality at the opera house. Rawdon and Becky make use of every opportunity in this new world, and Becky lays on the charm with the great and the good. George is increasingly captivated by Becky, who plays with his affections, all of which is noticed by Amelia with mounting dread. The cream of society go to a grand ball and George hands Becky a letter declaring his feelings for her. General Tufto announces that Napoleon is marching on Brussels and the men must leave immediately. Suddenly there's the sound of bugles and drums as the enemy crosses the river. George goes to Amelia, realising that he is a fool and has made a terrible mistake. After their tender parting, Amelia is distraught and confronts Becky about her treachery with George, saying, 'Leave me. I cannot bear the sight of you.' Cannon fire and rumbling is heard in the distance and conflicting reports about the battle filter back to the city.

War beckons

OUR YOUNG HEROES travel from the Kent coast to Brussels where, with Wellington and the rest of the British army gathered in the city or in fields near by, they await to engage with Napoleon. The allies – Britain, Russia, Austria and Prussia – have each vowed to maintain 150,000 men in the field, with the aim to overthrow Napoleon, who was now in Paris. By the spring of 1815 the allied armies were scattered across Europe: the Prussian army under Marshal Blücher was on the borders of Holland and Germany; the Austrian army was in northern Italy, should Napoleon attack

there; the Russians were in Poland; and the British, Dutch, Belgian and German forces, under Wellington, were stationed in and around Brussels. No one knew where exactly Napoleon's 125,000-strong army would attack first; Napoleon was skilful in concealing his movements by spreading false information and sealing the French borders. It was a case of waiting to see what his next move would be, and it was not until early June that the allies learned that Napoleon had reached the Belgian border, having previously been unaware that he had left Paris.

Dancing and feasting

Over the ten-week wait in and around Brussels, the troops had plenty of ways to amuse themselves. Like Becky and Amelia, many wives accompanied their officer husbands, along with hundreds of sightseers. By the summer of 1815 Brussels was packed with members of high society – it was quite the place to be, as Thackeray describes in the novel: 'There never was, since the days of Darius, such a brilliant train of camp-followers as hung round the Duke of Wellington's army in the Low Countries, in 1815; and led it dancing and feasting, as it were, up to the very brink of battle.'

To keep up morale, a host of entertainments were laid on. Wellington himself was said to have arranged grand dinners and balls, the Whig politician and diarist Thomas Creevey writing that 'the Duke during this period was forever giving balls … and very agreeable they were'. There were also cricket matches and horse-races, fox-hunts in the local forests, musical events, operas and

A key scene in Brussels is set in a restaurant. To modern audiences, this might not seem out of the ordinary, but in 1815 and even as late as 1850 the whole concept would have been unfamiliar to the British. Restaurants had first appeared in Paris in the late eighteenth century as an alternative to crowded, often unhygienic taverns, and a number of luxury establishments with elaborately prepared dishes opened in Paris towards the end of the century.

picnics. In *Vanity Fair*, George Osborne takes the opportunity presented at Brussels to mingle with 'the quality', such as Lady Bareacres, her daughter Lady Blanche and the countless aristocrats who had arrived in Brussels. Wellington, having sent his wife Kitty back to England from Paris in March, was entertained by various English ladies, including Lady Shelley and Lady Frances Wedderburn-Webster, whose husband would later sue a newspaper for suggesting his wife had had an affair with the Duke.

A popular entertainment put on for the officers and their wives in Brussels was the opera. In *Vanity Fair*, the opera serves almost as background music to the real drama going on in the auditorium: the flirtatious interaction between Becky, George and General Tufto. This was a not-uncommon experience in opera houses during the period, as Dr Ambrogio Caiani, historian and an adviser to the series, explains: 'Some opera audiences were incredibly badly behaved; they would be chatting away, people might even cook food behind the boxes, so the performers would almost have to fight for their attention. The staging would have been far more over-the-top than we see today, with performers gesticulating wildly and playing up the drama as much as possible. For many, the opera was a place to meet people and be seen, and wasn't just about the musical performance.'

The music in the scene is from *Così fan tutte*. First performed in 1790, Mozart's opera takes a cynical swipe at fidelity, the relationship between men and women, and how the latter are often untrustworthy – a gentle nod and warning, perhaps, to those caught up in Becky's schemes.

The Duchess of Richmond's Ball, by Robert Alexander Hillingford.

The dancing and feasting at Brussels would continue right up until the very brink of battle. One such ball, that of the Duchess of Richmond, forms a major scene in *Vanity Fair*. Known as the 'most famous ball in history', it was held on 15 June, the day before Quatre Bras and just three days before the Battle of Waterloo itself. Almost every senior officer in Wellington's army attended, including the Duke himself, and it caused great excitement, as Thackeray writes: 'All Brussels had been in a state of excitement about it, and I have heard from the ladies who were in the town at the period, that the talk and interest of persons of their own sex regarding the ball was much greater even than in respect of enemy in their front.'

Unaware just how close Napoleon's army was to Brussels, the Duke of Wellington, just as he sat down to supper, received word that the French had swept through Charleroi, only fifty kilometres south of Brussels, earlier in the day. Like Rawdon, George and Dobbin, half the guests were immediately forced to leave the ball and join their regiments, although according to the Dowager Lady de Ros, in her 'Personal Recollections of the Great Duke of Wellington', some of the officers stayed on at the ball and had to fight the next day in evening costume.

As in *Vanity Fair*, Brussels would have woken up to the sound of horses' hooves and wagons, soldiers assembling and taking an emotional leave of their families before marching off to battle.

Wellington's army

THE DUKE OF Wellington's army consisted of around sixty-eight thousand men, twenty-five thousand of whom were British, with the rest made of Germans and Dutch-Belgians. Only seven thousand men were veterans of the Peninsular War; the rest had to be recruited, often from county militias and yeomanry regiments. Of the British soldiers, many were Scottish and an even larger number – around 38 per cent – hailed from Ireland, explaining perhaps the inclusion of the characters Colonel and Lady O'Dowd in *Vanity Fair*.

Almost all officers in the British army, particularly those in the higher ranks, came from the aristocracy or landed gentry, with a few from the professional classes, and many bought their commissions. It's likely that the families of George and Rawdon would have purchased their commissions; Wellington himself, the son of the Earl of Mornington, had originally bought his way in. Officer ranks were often traded, although during the later years of the Napoleonic Wars more promotions were given on merit: both Dobbin and Rawdon are raised to the rank of colonel after Waterloo. Soldiers could expect to spend long periods abroad, such as in the Caribbean and India, where indeed Dobbin and Jos are sent with their regiment.

WILLIAM DOBBIN

A CHARACTER WHO doesn't perhaps stand out as much as some of the more flashy types is Captain William Dobbin. Impossibly shy and a little awkward, he is nonetheless reliable and sturdy, as his cart-horse name might suggest. 'He's not as glamorous as the others,' says series writer Gwyneth Hughes. 'He's a bit stiff, a bit unimaginative, but he's utterly virtuous and so lovely and kind. He's all heart and all man, and if anyone's the hero in *Vanity Fair*, it's Dobbin.'

Johnny Flynn, who plays Dobbin, agrees: 'He's not as exciting as some of the other characters, and his name is Dobbin for a reason. But unlike everyone else, he's constantly thinking and doing things for other people and he doesn't act out of selfish want. He's really the only thoroughly decent character in the story.'

Dobbin is a soldier and gentleman, a former school pal of George Osborne, whom he protected from bullies, and he remains a true and steadfast friend. From the outset, we know that Dobbin is deeply in love with Amelia Sedley, who is engaged to George. The tension born out of that seemingly impossible situation is a central thread in *Vanity Fair* – one that holds our attention and sympathy throughout.

JOHNNY FLYNN: This was a time that, for the gentrified class, the important thing was empire, being a soldier and wearing ridiculous clothes, proud, upright, chivalric and decent. I've never had to do that for a part. I really liked thinking about that.

Out of love for Amelia, who he can see is besotted with George, Dobbin constantly cajoles George to show more affection to his betrothed and is instrumental in ensuring they marry. It's an utterly selfless act, and we can feel his pain even if he never openly voices it. He continually pleads with Mr Osborne to sanction the union and throughout supports Amelia with his friendship, buying her much-loved piano when her father is made bankrupt (unbeknownst to Amelia, who assumes George had bought it for her), and supporting her financially when she is widowed and bears a son.

'Dobbin really is a steadfast friend, someone you can rely on,' says Johnny. 'He crops up intermittently in the story and often doesn't say much, but he's there at the Battle of Waterloo, he brings Amelia and George together, and then of course there's this really heroic moment in Germany, when he comes back through the mist on a boat to be with Amelia.'

'I knew that Gwyneth had always thought of Dobbin as the hero of the story,' Johnny continues, 'and I wrestled with that because how do you play someone who is heroic, but in a chivalric, Arthurian kind of way? He's decent, solid and he's full of love and compassion and never does anything for himself. It takes a long time for his story to play out – it's almost as if that's what Thackeray intended, as if he is saying that those who wait reap the rewards.'

Johnny Flynn, who has appeared in a variety of theatre, television and film roles, from the Channel 4 and Netflix sitcom *Lovesick* to the hit play *Jerusalem*, is also a composer and singer-songwriter in the band Johnny Flynn & The Sussex Wit. Getting to grips with the role of Dobbin was an interesting process for Johnny: 'When I play a character, I write a list of all the things we have in common, and then I have to imagine all the other stuff. With Dobbin, there was quite a lot I could connect with. In the novel, we learn that he's a grocer's son and a scholarship boy at school – and his fellow pupils mock him mercilessly over his tradesman father. I was also a scholarship boy and didn't come from a wealthy background, unlike a lot of my peers at school, so I could relate to that.

'There's humility with Dobbin that I like. His love for Amelia is also interesting, and almost a little weird. Most people don't hang on like that; it's slightly obsessive and she's not really complicit in the relationship until the end.'

When it comes to Becky, Dobbin is one of the few characters who is immune to her charms, whilst almost everyone else is taken in. 'He's so decent, though,' says Johnny, 'that he's not going to wade in and be rude her. It's only later on in the story, when Becky turns up in Amelia's life in Pumpernickel, that he warns Amelia about Becky – that she's deceived her before – and that's what causes a rift between Amelia and Dobbin.'

BECKY

Dear heaven, Amelia, if I had the chance of a man with a heart as big as his, and the brains to match – I'd overlook his big feet.

This rift ultimately leads to Dobbin coming to the realisation that he has deluded himself about Amelia, that in fact she might not be a prize worth winning. He fears that Amelia's blind worship of her dead husband shows that her soul is shallow and that she can 'never feel love as deep as mine. As real as mine.' His outburst jolts Amelia into action and she finally see the man in front of her, even before Becky has revealed the full extent of George's unfaithfulness. Amelia and Dobbin do finally marry, although it's clear Dobbin does so with open eyes, and they have a daughter, Janey. Amelia recognises that Janey is now the love of Dobbin's life, and this brings him the happiness he deserves.

Gwyneth Hughes agrees that Dobbin is really the kind of husband we should all have, rather than the raffish cads that all the young women seem to go for in *Vanity Fair*. As Johnny reminds us, 'This is not a neat story, these are messy lives and crazy things happen to people in *Vanity Fair*. If Dobbin didn't exist, you wouldn't know how mad everyone else is.

'For me, *Vanity Fair* is an amazing, colourful tale in which all these unlikely characters are like spinning tops, thrust out into a carnival-like environment, and they keep bumping into each other. These people destroy each other, fall in love with each other, and lead these mad young lives, yet Dobbin remains constant and dignified, and shows everyone for what they are. Everyone else wants to get on in life, make money, be glamorous. Dobbin doesn't do any of that, he just is.'

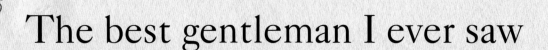

The best gentleman I ever saw

A CENTRAL THEME in *Vanity Fair* is what it is to be a man, and in particular a gentleman. *Vanity Fair* swarms with male characters, all of whom have their own ideas about what makes a gentleman: some think that only those with blue blood and pedigree can be called one; others dress in fine clothes, travel in carriages and fraternise with the fashionable; some engage in what they see as masculine pursuits ('See the chaps in a boat-race; look at the fellers in a fight; aye, look at a dawg killing rats—which is it wins? the good-blooded ones' says one character in the novel in summation of what it is to be a gentleman), drink (but only such beverages as port or claret, never stout, as Jos claims at Vauxhall), gamble and indulge in an array of vain pleasures thought proper for a real man. Others, and we can assume Thackeray fell into this category, believe that a gentleman is made by personality and character. Dobbin, who in the novel was bullied as a child for having a grocer father, because 'the selling of goods by retail is a shameful and infamous practice, meriting the contempt and scorn of all real gentlemen', is in fact the only true gentleman, a rarity in the fickle world of *Vanity Fair*. In Thackeray's own words:

We all know a hundred whose coats are very well made, and a score who have excellent manners, and one or two happy beings who are what they call in the inner circles, and have shot in the very centre and bull's-eye of the fashion; but of gentlemen how many? … Let us take a scrap of paper and each make out his list. My friend the Major I write, without any doubt, in mine … his thoughts were just, his brains were fairly good, his life was honest and pure, and his heart warm and humble.

Ensign Stubble practising the art of war with Captain Dobbin.

Unrequited love

THE EMOTIONAL HEART of *Vanity Fair* lies in Dobbin's long-suffering love for Amelia, a woman who is betrothed and then married to another man. Thackeray may well have identified with Dobbin's plight as he was in a similar situation during the conception and writing of the novel.

Thackeray had married his young wife Isabella Shawe in 1836. After having a daughter, Anne, they moved from Paris back to Bloomsbury. Money was tight and Thackeray worked long hours as a journalist and writer. Another daughter died in infancy in 1839 and financial pressure forced Thackeray into more and more work. Isabella was suffering increasingly from isolation and depression, a situation that worsened after the birth of a third daughter, Harriet, in 1840. She became both restless and apathetic, with alarmed nervousness that descended into 'absolute insanity', as Thackeray put it, when, on a boat trip to see Isabella's mother in Ireland, she jumped into the sea. She never recovered, and for several years Thackeray shuttled between London and Paris, where his parents and children were, and his wife, who was in a series of asylums in France. Thackeray eventually brought Isabella back to England in 1845 and she lived with an associate of his mother's in Camberwell. Isabella then more or less fades from view, largely because Thackeray rarely spoke or wrote about his wife.

In 1846 Thackeray established a home for himself and his daughters in Kensington. During the difficult years of the 1840s, he had found solace in visiting the house of an old Cambridge friend, William Brookfield, where he met and quickly formed an attachment to his wife, Jane. In letters to her, Thackeray professes his devotion, which

Jane Brookfield

Virtue is rewarded: Thackeray's illustration for the final instalment of *Vanity Fair*.

she appears to accept but, like Amelia with Dobbin, she strings him along for years. Jane claimed her husband was unsympathetic to her and Thackeray certainly felt William treated his wife with coldness and neglect, as George Osborne did to Amelia, and years later berated William for it. Ultimately, however, Jane remained loyal to her husband and would send Thackeray chilled letters if her husband complained of their friendship. In 1846, Thackeray admitted to his mother, 'I have been in love with her these four years', and in other letters described how he was half mad with love. In 1847, when it was mooted that the Brookfields move in with Thackeray as a result of financial difficulties, Thackeray vetoed the plan, acknowledging 'loving her as I do … *that* would be dangerous, and so I keep off'.

During the writing of the novel, Thackeray was still infatuated with Jane and this may well have influenced the shaping of Dobbin's character and his increasing frustration and disenchantment with Amelia. After completing *Vanity Fair*, he had grown tired of the tense emotional triangle, and by 1852 had parted company with the Brookfields. In the novel, Amelia sees the error of her ways and marries Dobbin, an ending that Thackeray may have wished for himself while he was writing.

Some think that Dobbin is essentially Thackeray – they share the same forename, suffer the same unrequited love, and Thackeray's deepest personal feelings seem to speak through him. The writer appears to reserve a particular fondness for his character, referring to him in the novel as 'dear captain Dobbin' or 'my friend the major'. Dobbin was in fact a late inclusion: he didn't feature in the first few chapters submitted to the publisher Colburn in 1845. Between Colburn rejecting the novel and Bradbury & Evans agreeing to bring it out in monthly parts there was an eight-month hiatus, during which Thackeray introduced Dobbin, an addition that served to give the novel its emotional core.

Thackeray also confessed to his mother that he probably made Amelia like Jane and told William Brookfield that, although Amelia was not a copy of his wife, he could not have conceived the character had he not known her. Aware of this, Jane expressed her wish that the character of Amelia was more exciting as, in her view, she was exceedingly dull – contrary to the critics, who raved about Amelia as the epitome of Victorian womanhood.

CHAPTER

FIVE

In which battles are won and lost

---

*I love Rawdon and he
loves me, but I never wanted
to be a mother*

THE MEN MARCH towards battle surrounded by retreating wounded soldiers. The French cavalry charge and run through the ragged English mob. Ensign Stubble is wounded. In Brussels, Jos buys Becky's horses for a huge sum and escapes the city, while Amelia waits in sheer terror. The French fire artillery and charge at the British infantry as Dobbin and George stand inside a defensive square, commanding their men. The French retreat and General Tufto is shot while surveying the scene with Rawdon. Hundreds of the French Imperial Guard appear as the British lie in wait for them. The British fire, there's carnage and the French flee.

As British troops march forward, George is shot in the heart and killed. Some weeks after, Mr Osborne visits the site of his son's death. Amelia is bereft and Dobbin tries to convince Mr Osborne to reconcile with Amelia, who is now carrying his grandchild. Later, Dobbin visits Amelia and baby Georgy with news that he is to leave for India. Rawdon, Becky and baby Rawdy visit ailing Aunt Matilda, who dies as she rails against them. Becky, needing another financial plan, sets up a gaming room in their new lodgings in Mayfair. Mr Osborne writes to Amelia saying he'll take in Georgy and make him his heir, which Amelia refuses. Lord Steyne pays a visit.

Quatre Bras

Officers salute Mrs O'Dowd, Amelia and Jos before they head to battle.

OUR YOUNG OFFICERS now leave Brussels and head towards battle, with Dobbin, George and Major O'Dowd riding at the head of their marching battalion. A drummer sets the rhythm and a standard-bearer carries the regimental colours. As they march they come across exhausted, wounded soldiers sitting and lying at the side of the road; a badly injured horse is shot – the scene does not bode well for the battle ahead.

The marching battalion is heading to the crossroads at Quatre Bras, where an intense battle has been raging with the French. The scene is based on the very real events leading up to the Battle of Waterloo. Napoleon's army had crossed into what is now Belgium, forming a twenty-kilometre front

The troops in *Vanity Fair* march to the beat of a drum, as was common in the Napoleonic Wars. Drums were an integral part of the British army, used on the battlefield, where officers' commands could be misheard, to give orders; a specified drumroll might communicate a change of formation, or when to advance or retreat. Drummers were often very young: at least one drummer at Waterloo was fourteen, although only about 10 per cent of the 304 British drummers at Waterloo were under sixteen.

that separated the British and Prussian forces. To force open the road to Brussels at Quatre Bras, Napoleon had dispatched a corps under the command of Marshal Ney. Napoleon himself led the bulk of his forces towards the Prussians, around seven kilometres to the east, at Ligny.

Ney's force of eighteen thousand men, which included two thousand cavalry and thirty-two guns, faced a Dutch-Belgian force of just eight thousand infantry and sixteen guns under the command of William, Prince of Orange. They repelled Ney's initial attack on the morning of 16 June 1815, but were gradually driven back by the overwhelming number of French troops. Reinforcements began to arrive in the afternoon and the Duke of Wellington took command. The allies were able to drive Ney's forces back and secure the crossroads by the evening, though casualties were high: the allies lost 4700 men, the French 4300. The allies were unable to help the Prussians, who had already been defeated by the French. Blücher lost some sixteen thousand men at the Battle of Ligny.

Much of the fighting at Quatre Bras occurred in and around the Bossu Wood, where George and Dobbin's regiment are suddenly set upon by Napoleon's forces. The infantry try to form a defensive square but they're too late: the sabre-wielding French cavalry is upon them. From horseback, George fires his pistol and kills a French officer, as does Dobbin, but Ensign Stubble is wounded by a French cavalryman.

The regiment's standard-bearer is killed in the mêlée. Ensign Stubble then lifts the standard and waves it aloft, before he is struck by a French sabre. When a flag-bearer was killed, it was the duty of any survivors to carry it. Losing the standard not only meant the troop had lost its visual point to rally around, but it was also seen as a loss of honour for the unit. By picking up the flag, Stubble was bravely doing his duty, although this no doubt made him more of a target for the enemy.

The Battle of Waterloo

WE NEXT SEE General Tufto and Captain Rawdon Crawley poring over a map, having been given orders to march to Waterloo. After Quatre Bras, the British moved northwards, positioning themselves behind a ridge at Mont-Saint-Jean, to the south of the village of Waterloo. Knowing that the allies were marginally outnumbered by the French and nervous about their chances in open battle, Wellington initially established a strong defensive position, blocking the road to Brussels in order to stop Napoleon's advance to the city. The weather had turned wet and rain poured down on the troops, who were forced to camp out in the open. This wet weather, however, was to prove crucial, as not only did it drench the enemy now camping out close by, but it also forced Napoleon to delay his attack as it was difficult to move artillery over boggy ground. At the same time, Blücher's Prussian forces were marching north-west to link up with Wellington's men.

Keen to engage Wellington before the Prussians arrived, Napoleon finally began his attack on 18 June 1815. Napoleon repeatedly threw his columns against the bayonet-wielding British infantry and for a time it looked as if the British would give way under the onslaught. By around three o'clock in the afternoon, the first Prussian troops had

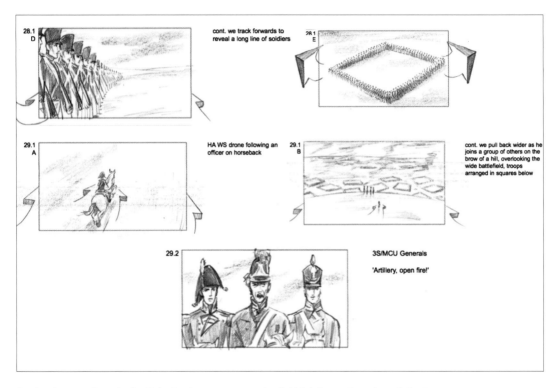

Production storyboards detail the battle sequence, as the British infantry form into defensive squares.

begun to arrive, while the allied forces continued to come under sustained artillery bombardment. At around four, thinking that Wellington's front was weakening, the French decided to launch a series of cavalry charges against the centre of the allied infantry line.

The British infantry responded by forming into defensive squares, a scene viewed in the series by General Tufto and Captain Crawley from a hilltop above. The square is four rows deep; the front row kneels, the second crouches, both with bayonets fixed. Lines three and four stand, the fourth without bayonets. All await the order to fire, which will come from Dobbin and George, who stand inside the square along with Major O'Dowd.

The French cannon fire gets closer, and soon some of the men in the front line are blown backwards. The injured are moved into the centre of the square; Dobbin heroically runs forward and drags an injured man into the centre just as the French cavalrymen approach the square. At the last possible moment, the order to fire is given – the first row fire and French horses fall; the second row fire to the same effect and French officers, now without their horses, charge but are shot and bayoneted. From his vantage point, General Tufto announces that the French are in retreat, just before he is shot in the head and killed. (Many senior officers lost their lives at Waterloo, including General Thomas Picton, who received a bullet through the temple as he shouted at his troops to charge the French early on in the battle.)

Captain Dobbin, at the last moment, heroically saves a wounded soldier and takes him back into the infantry square.

PAUL BIDDISS, military adviser to *Vanity Fair*: The defensive square was a very effective defence against cavalry. The officer on horseback might be willing to push forward but the horse, faced with a lot of shiny bayonets, will just stop and rear up. In this way the squares were almost impenetrable, although they were vulnerable to cannon fire.

At Waterloo, the French cavalry would regroup and charge again and again over three hours, but the squares failed to cave and artillery teams emerged from them to fire in between attacks. At around six o'clock the French launched a combined cavalry and infantry attack in a renewed effort to capture the farm of La Haye Sainte, in the middle of the battlefield. This time they were successful, and now the centre of the allied line was open to a full French assault.

At approximately seven o'clock, Marshal Ney led a column of six thousand men of the Imperial Guard, Napoleon's finest unit, to La Haye Sainte. What happened next forms the final battle scene in *Vanity Fair*. As they head up the ridge, the Imperial

Guard appear out of thick mist, marching to the beat of their drums. Out of sight, on the other side of the slope, lie hundreds of British troops, including George and Dobbin. As the French get closer, the British battalion stand all at once, like ghosts in the mist. Just as the Imperial Guard are upon them, the first rank fire and the front rows of the French fall, then the second rank fire, and it's carnage. The French are decimated but continue to fight, then eventually they turn to flee. George, elated, advances with Dobbin, but as he shouts 'Now is our time!' he is shot through the heart and falls to the ground, dead.

As the survivors of the Imperial Guard fled, it was clear to French troops in the rear that the battle was lost and a full-scale withdrawal began. As the enemy retreated, the Prussians chased them – the rest of the allied troops were exhausted after nine hours of battle. Napoleon himself was forced to abandon his carriage and within days would abdicate and then surrender to the British.

'Up Guards and at them!': the rout of Napoleon's Imperial Guard.

It came at last: the columns of the Imperial Guard marched up the hill of Saint Jean, at length and at once to sweep the English from the height which they had maintained all day, and spite of all; unscared by the thunder of the artillery, which hurled death from the English line—the dark rolling column pressed on and up the hill. It seemed almost to crest the eminence, when it began to wave and falter. Then it stopped, still facing the shot. Then at last the English troops rushed from the post from which no enemy had been able to dislodge them and the Guard turned and fled.

No more firing was heard at Brussels— the pursuit rolled miles away. Darkness came down on the field and city: and Amelia was praying for George, who was lying on his face, dead, with a bullet through his heart.

The overwhelming victory had been won at heavy cost: Wellington's casualties numbered fifteen thousand and Blücher's eight thousand. Napoleon lost twenty-five thousand men killed and wounded and nine thousand captured. The rolling farmland south of Brussels was full of dead and dying troops. On learning of the casualty lists, the Duke of Wellington is reported to have remarked, 'I always say that, next to a battle lost, the greatest misery is a battle gained.'

CLOCKWISE FROM TOP LEFT:

The French cavalry charge as Dobbin rescues a wounded infantryman.

The standard uniform for the majority of regiments in 1815 was the traditional red coat. Rank-and-file soldiers wore white cotton duck or grey woollen trousers and a shako. Officers were responsible for providing their own uniforms and so varied in style, though infantry officers generally wore white pantaloons tucked into boots, and scarlet coatees (short coats).

Ensign Stubble receives a wound to the shoulder at Quatre Bras.

The Imperial Guard wore bearskin hats. After seeing them at Waterloo, the Duke of Wellington introduced them to Britain and they are still worn by Guards regiments today.

PAUL BIDDISS: This kind of combat resulted in a lot of fatalities, particularly from cannon fire, with solid steel cannon balls that would go right through you and into the next man. Some of the cannons fired explosives or rockets but most shot solid steel projectiles.

To recreate the Battle of Waterloo, the series creators and military advisers researched contemporary battlefield manuals and memoirs of the time. This one details a soldier's experiences of lying on the reverse slope, hearing the Imperial Guard coming forward, and how, as the French are forced back, Lord Saltoun shouts 'Now's the time, my boys', just as George does in *Vanity Fair*.

Captain H. W. Powell, First Foot Guards

There ran along this part of the position a cart road, on one side of which was a ditch and bank, in and under which the Brigade sheltered themselves during the cannonade, which might have lasted three-quarters of an hour. Without the protection of this bank every creature must have perished.

The Emperor probably calculated on this effect, for suddenly the firing ceased, and as the smoke cleared away a most superb sight opened on us. A close Column of Grenadiers (about seventies in front) of la Moyenne Garde, about 6,000 strong, led, as we have since heard, by Marshal Ney, were seen ascending the rise au pas de charge shouting 'Vive I'Empereur'. They continued to advance till within fifty or sixty paces of our front, when the Brigade were ordered to stand up. Whether it was from the sudden appearance of a Corps so near them, which must have seemed as starting out of the ground, or the tremendously heavy fire we threw into them, La Garde, who had never before failed in an attack suddenly stopped. Those who from a distance and more on the flank could see the affair, tell us that the effect of our fire seemed to force the head of the Column bodily back.

In less than a minute above 300 were down. They now wavered, and several of the rear divisions began to draw out as if to deploy, whilst some of the men in their rear beginning to fire over the heads of those in front was so evident proof of their confusion, that Lord Saltoun (who had joined the Brigade, having had the whole of his Light Infantry Battalion dispersed at Hougoumont) holloaed out, 'Now's the time, my boys'. Immediately the Brigade sprang forward. La Garde turned and gave us little opportunity of trying the steel. We charged down the hill till we had passed the end of the orchard of Hougoumont, when our right flank became exposed to another heavy Column (as we afterwards understood of the Chasseurs of the Garde) who were advancing in support of the former Column. This circumstance, besides that our charge was isolated, obliged the Brigade to retire towards their original position.

Victory

News of the victory at Waterloo reached London late on 21 June, and by 26 June the papers had announced Napoleon's abdication. Many were relieved that the conflict was finally at an end, that a tyrant had once and for all been removed from Europe, although some were saddened to see the downfall of their hero and celebrations were mixed with mourning for all those who had died. Napoleon would spend the remainder of his life in exile on the island of St Helena in the South Atlantic. Louis XVIII was restored to the French throne on 7 July and the subsequent Treaty of Paris reduced France's borders to those of 1790 and required France to pay an indemnity of 700 million francs.

A medal engraved by Benedetto Pistrucci to commemorate the victory at Waterloo.

This final defeat of Napoleon marked a turning point in history, as although there were a great many wars across the continent throughout the century, France's domination of Europe had come to an end. The French turned their attention to building their empire across Africa, while Britain's global ambitions remained very much intact.

After Waterloo, some 350,000 serving men returned to Britain – one in six of the male population aged between fifteen and forty. For the rank and file, many of whom were wounded and without pensions, unemployment and hardship lay ahead,

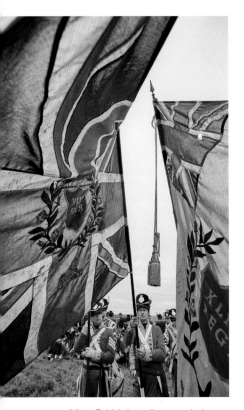

Most British battalions carried two flags, known as colours: one the Union flag with the regiment's number in the centre surrounded by a wreath, and the second in the colour of the regiment's facings, with a Union flag in the corner and regimental number in the centre. The colours above represent the 44th Regiment of Foot, the infantry regiment of George and Dobbin, but also a real regiment that saw service throughout the Napoleonic Wars and at Waterloo.

a situation exacerbated by poor weather, failed harvests and continuing high food prices, which would culminate in political unrest. Nonetheless, the constant threat of invasion during the wars, mass mobilisation and adversity in the face of a common foe had fostered a certain spirit of unity and national feeling, and Thackeray was fascinated by this. Wellington ensured that those who had fought at Waterloo all received a campaign medal – the first time the government had awarded a medal to soldiers for an action regardless of rank – and many servicemen carried theirs for the rest of their lives.

Some viewed the victory at Waterloo as a source of national pride, commemorated and celebrated for decades afterwards. Many, however, mourned its huge loss of life and the suffering inflicted on working people, which would result in discontent with the state rather than any lasting sense of national unity. Thackeray himself denounced the triumphalism inspired by war and saw little glory in death on the battlefield, writing in 1841, 'Accursed be all uniform coats, guns, shrapnels, musketoons … What right have I to plume myself because the Duke of Wellington beat the French in Spain?'

Filming the battle

THACKERAY DID NOT write about the battles in any great detail in the novel of *Vanity Fair*, preferring instead to focus on those left behind in Brussels, who would be so deeply affected by events. While for some people in Britain the Napoleonic Wars were a distant rumble, most were touched by the conflict in some way, losing loved ones or living under the threat of invasion or financial uncertainty.

The makers of the series, however, were keen to dramatise key parts of the Battle of Waterloo, as producer Julia Stannard explains: 'While Thackeray chose not to write about the battle, we had the opportunity to visualise and dramatise it. We did discuss whether we should include it as our key characters aren't there, but of course their lives are affected by it dramatically; both Becky and Amelia are drawn into the vortex of war. But the battle is such a pivotal moment in our story – it's the death of one of our main characters and to deny the audience that would be wrong. We decided to go for it and do it properly and big. So you see Dobbin, Rawdon and George right in the middle of the battle.'

Overseeing the filming of the Battle of Waterloo and the whole production is *Vanity Fair*'s director James Strong: 'This is a big production for ITV and Amazon Studios – event television – and to achieve that we need to use the very latest technology. My job as a director is to make sure the series achieves the scale and vision that people expect. It should feel like a film, a full cinematic experience – viewers want a spectacle.'

'Many of those fighting, like George and Dobbin, were young men in their twenties, who had lived privileged, cossetted lives,' Julia continues. 'Life then becomes very real and they're suddenly in the line of fire. George says on the eve of battle that he never thought it would actually happen, and there he is with cavalry charging and guns firing. That juxtaposition – the safe world of London society and the battlefield – that's what it was to live as a young man in those times.'

Shooting the battle sequences was a huge undertaking for the creators of the series, involving hundreds of supporting artists (one hundred of whom were re-enactors), a large number of horses, including a team of Spanish stunt horses and riders, military advisers, special-effects technicians and an enormous production crew who have to mobilise, organise, dress and equip the extras and actors, not to mention film all the action. Once everything is shot, further CGI (computer-generated imagery) then builds the battlefield to an even greater extent, adding more people, extra explosions and further texture to recreate the battle that involved two hundred thousand men.

Boot camp

The filming of the battle sequences required three hundred supporting artists to stand in for the British army. Two hundred of these extras were specially trained at a boot camp in order to get them ready for the particular demands of filming. The series military adviser Paul Biddiss, himself a former serviceman, oversaw the boot camps and explains what went into the training:

'Most of the guys we trained had never touched a weapon in their lives. In essence, we were training them to be British soldiers at the Battle of Waterloo, to perform various drills and movements as they would have done in 1815. Our job was to get them ready for filming, so that when the director asked them to do something they could do it immediately, without wasting a lot of time (and money!)

'Drill was essential for a British soldier, along with the controlled firing of muskets in formation. Well-drilled soldiers could get into a

defensive formation more quickly and efficiently, with a faster rate of fire.

'On the first day of training, each extra was taught about their equipment, what it was for and how it was worn. This meant they knew how to dress themselves, which in turn saved lots of time during filming. We then moved on to drill movements, teaching the men how to march in a straight line, how to get into battle formations of lines and columns, and how to advance quickly into a defensive square, which was crucial if you were to face a French cavalry attack. For a large body of men, these manoeuvres are very difficult and we trained them so they could perform each movement and drill in time and as one body of men.

'We then moved on to bayonet training, how to charge in line with a bayonet on the end of a musket, and the armoury department taught each extra how to correctly load and fire a live musket.

'It wasn't just about marching and formations, though: we needed them to look the part and to imagine what it was like to look into the face of the enemy. We'd talk to them about the charge and their "war face". Some of the soldiers at Waterloo were incredibly brave; many wouldn't have wanted to be there, or were frightened or angry, but you had no choice but to keep fighting.'

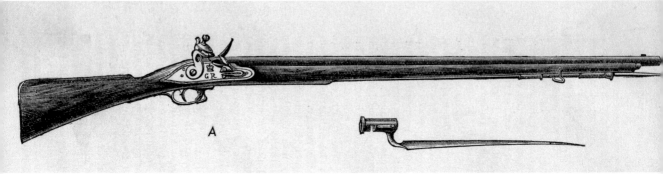

A

Musket fire

The British Army used India Pattern muskets, nicknamed the Brown Bess. Firing solid lead balls, the musket was effective at about forty metres and was capable of reaching beyond a hundred metres, although they were not accurate over long distances. Most engagements at this time, however, involved lines of soldiers, usually two deep, firing synchronised volleys at fairly close range. As Tony Browne, one of the armourers, explains: 'The soldiers at the time were really well trained, so they could load and fire three shots every minute – which is why the British army were such a good fighting force.'

The musket had a flintlock system, so to load it required putting black powder in the pan of the musket – the firing mechanism – and some down the barrel in the chamber with the charge. When the trigger is pulled, a piece of flint is brought down against a steel striker, producing sparks, which ignite the powder in the pan. As there is a hole going from the pan through to the barrel, the charge inside the chamber is then ignited, shooting the ball out of the barrel.

'For the filming, we put in normal black powder but not too much,' says Tony, 'and then some wadding down there to make

sure the powder stays in, so that when the musket is fired we get explosions and smoke. The muskets do occasionally misfire because the flint doesn't cause a spark or there's a blockage between the pan and the chamber, so on these shoots we try to keep the rifles as clean as possible. Back in 1815 the soldiers used their own personal weapons and they'd look after them really well, so there wouldn't have been so many misfires. The guns we've used are all replica guns; sometimes re-enactors have their own weapons, and we used the occasional dummy weapon that doesn't fire.'

Battle souvenirs

Back in Brussels, which was just twelve miles from the battlefield, the rumbling of cannon fire could easily be heard. The wounded were brought back into the city and conflicting rumours circulated about who had the upper hand – in the series, Jos's servant Isidor is convinced the 'rosbifs are finished'. As with Jos, some fled northwards in the belief that the French were about to triumphantly enter the city and many kept their horses close by so they could escape if Napoleon won the day.

In *Vanity Fair*, Becky's attention is caught by a market trader who, even before the battle has finished, is selling souvenirs from Waterloo. This mirrors the reality, as relic-hunters immediately scavenged the battlefield for anything valuable. Soldiers were often the first to pick through the

MARKET TRADER

Epaulets, plumes, straight from the battlefield. The blood still warm on some of this Dutch and German stuff.

BECKY

I only want French ones.

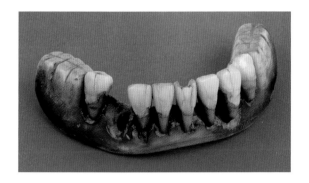

dead and wounded, followed by camp followers and local inhabitants. Some even came armed with pliers, as teeth from the dead were in high demand and could be made into dentures. So many dentures were made they were known as 'Waterloo teeth', and were popular because they were guaranteed to come from young, healthy soldiers.

In *Vanity Fair*, we see Mr Osborne visiting the battlefield some weeks after Waterloo and he's accosted by hawkers – or 'vultures', as he describes them – who are selling souvenirs. In reality, sightseers flocked there along with the scavengers, some even before the dead were buried, with visitors using snuff and brandy

to disguise the smell of rotting flesh. Writers and artists were also drawn to the site described by Lord Byron as the 'place of skulls': the poet William Wordsworth visited with his wife that summer, and Byron himself toured the ground the following year and purchased a sword, plumed helmet and breastplate.

Lord Byron

GEORGE OSBORNE

CHARLIE ROWE: My sideburns were put on hair by hair for an hour every morning and then they'd come off in a minute and a half at the end of the day. They are George's way of showing off: look at my structured whiskers, everyone has them. I don't notice them, or feel them, which is good.

LIKE MANY OTHERS in *Vanity Fair*, George Osborne is young, foolish and hopelessly vain, a character who just begins to grow up as the story progresses, until his journey abruptly ends on a sodden battlefield by the side of his old friend Dobbin. It's a wretched end for one so young, no matter his many weaknesses.

Brought up in a prosperous London home, George, when we first meet him, cuts a dashing figure in his lieutenant's uniform. Self-obsessed and snobbish, he's got little going for him other than his 'ambrosial whiskers', as Thackeray describes them, and he can't resist taking a look at himself in the mirror whenever he walks into a room.

George is the product of his controlling and domineering father, a self-made man intent on making his son a gentleman. As a result, both are self-centred and money-orientated, and George has been brought up to think he is superior to others. He considers himself a player, one of the men, and likes to associate with Rawdon Crawley, with whom he drinks and gambles, although he tends to lose large sums of money to his friend, a more astute card player.

Playing the part of George is twenty-two-year-old Charlie Rowe, an actor who has starred in

films such as *The Golden Compass* and *Never Let Me Go*, and more recently the television medical comedy-drama *Red Band Society*. 'Playing someone like George really affects me on a day-to-day basis: I sometimes come home in a darker mood and I get annoyed with my friends more quickly than I did before I played George!' says Charlie.

'George is selfish, vain and pretty ignorant, and thinks he's the best person in the world,' he continues. 'But then he slowly starts to realise that his father is not the nicest person, and at that point starts to question his whole upbringing.'

Since childhood, it has been assumed that George will marry Amelia Sedley, who is blindly smitten with him, despite his many faults. While George loves Amelia, the lack of a chase bores him and he takes advantage of her unceasing affection. 'George just doesn't realise how lucky he is to have someone like Amelia,' says Charlie.

When Amelia's father gets into financial trouble, Mr Osborne orders George to cut off ties with Amelia. George is uncomfortable with this, but it is only through the encouragement of Dobbin that he eventually defies his father and elopes with Amelia.

After hearing of the marriage, Mr Sedley disowns George, sending him a very small cheque and writing that he never wants to see his son again. 'In effect, George runs off with a girl who hasn't got enough money, and as a result a father decides he no longer loves his son,' says Charlie. 'It's all so twisted, and for me sums up what *Vanity Fair* is all about.'

As soon they are married, George and Amelia head to Brussels, where the British army are preparing for battle. 'He marries his beautiful wife,' says Charlie, 'and things start to look up.' Then, in Brussels, George sees Becky, whom he once scorned for her lowly background, circulating with the top brass in the army. He starts clumsily trying to ingratiate himself with the high society that have

CHARLIE ROWE: Dobbin is George's best mate; I don't know why, because George is so horrible to him. Dobbin is George's saviour – he's like this angel sitting on George's shoulder, telling George what to do and to get his life in order.

flocked to Brussels, in particular the Bareacres who, despite George's efforts, sneer at him and his young wife.

At the same time, Becky begins to openly flirt with George, making eyes at him at the opera, which George foolishly misinterprets as a sign of real affection. 'Becky manipulates everyone around her, particularly the men, and does it masterfully with George,' says Charlie. 'There's a moment at the ball, just before the war is announced, when George tries to sweep Becky off her feet and dance with her. She's very flirtatious and gives him everything he wants in the conversation, although it's clearly just one of her ploys to extract more money from him. George believes Becky is in love with him and is prepared to abandon his wife for her. They're just as horrible as each other!'

Having written to Becky to say that he would run away with her, George is suddenly filled with genuine remorse as he and Dobbin prepare to head off to battle. The enormity of what he's about to face suddenly brings everything into sharp focus, and he can see he's made a huge mistake. 'Dobbin, I have ruined her life and mine,' George says. 'Emmy, dear God, so gentle and tender, when I've been so selfish, and brutal, and full of self-pity. I'm not fit to be a married man.' Again encouraged by Dobbin, George goes to Amelia and they spend a brief and final moment in each other's arms before he is taken away to war.

As series writer Gwyneth Hughes reminds us, 'George is very young and people in their early twenties are often selfish, self-obsessed and hopeless, but what's so sad is that he doesn't live long enough to become the good, kind grown-up he could have been.'

'George ends up in a worse place than anyone,' sums up Charlie. 'He's like the guy in a horror film who disappears first. He doesn't focus on what's important and he constantly makes mistake after bad mistake.'

CHARLIE ROWE: There are moments on a set when you realise just how lucky you are. The Battle of Waterloo was one of those moments, when you're on horseback holding a sword, with your friends, there's a massive crew, fifty Spanish stunt horses, just madness. The whole week of filming was great.

OPPOSITE: George in action at Quatre Bras.

CHAPTER

SIX

In which a painter's daughter meets a king

What a fine country we are, where a little governess may meet a king

---

SIR PITT CRAWLEY collapses and later dies. Lord Steyne pays Becky a visit, gives her a diamond necklace, and it's clear they are in the midst of some kind of tryst. The family assemble for Sir Pitt's funeral; Martha and Bute immediately take control of Queen's Crawley and sack servants Horrocks and Betsey. Amelia, still living in reduced circumstances, argues with her mother about medicine for Georgy and Mr Sedley invites Reverend Binny to discuss Georgy's education. Jos and Dobbin, meanwhile, are in India, where Mrs O'Dowd sets up her sister Glorvina as a match for Dobbin. Dressed in fabrics that Becky has stolen from Queen's Crawley, Becky and Rawdon are presented to the King. Amelia finally agrees to let Georgy live at the Osbornes' and she is full of despair. Becky and Rawdon are invited to a dinner party at Lord Steyne's, where the ladies treat Becky with scorn. Bailiffs catch up with Rawdon and he ends up at the sponging house. He writes to Becky asking her to repay the debt but gets no reply; his brother Bute comes to his aid. Rawdon, released, heads back to discover Becky with Lord Steyne. Rawdon throws Steyne to the floor, orders him out and hurls back all of Becky's trinkets. Rawdon leaves and Becky sits 'amidst the wreckage of her life'.

LORD STEYNE

What a clever little monkey it is, that can extract diamonds from one pocket and cash from another

---

BECKY SHARP MOVES into very dangerous territory when she allows Lord Steyne to enter her life. He is, as Becky puts it, 'one of the most important lords of the land', who even has the ear of the king when he is granted the coveted Court position of Master of the Powder Closet.

Immensely wealthy and influential, Lord Steyne is a perfect example of just how rotten those at the top of the social tree can be. In the words of Anthony Head, who plays Lord Steyne, 'He's a nasty piece of work.' When Becky catches his eye, Lord Steyne uses everything within his considerable means to procure her – and he's used to getting what he wants. He showers her with money and fine jewellery, which Becky accepts in the mistaken belief she can control the situation. 'In return for arranging for Becky to meet the King,' continues Anthony, 'Lord Steyne, like the devil, barters and buys her soul.'

Becky allows herself to be seduced by Lord Steyne, believing it to be the price she must pay for social advancement. At the same time, she

LADY STEYNE

They look at you with rage in their hearts. They look at me with pity. But they would change places with either of us in a minute. Your youth, and my wealth. Will you play for me?

and Lady Steyne form an unlikely alliance, while other high-society ladies continue to shun Becky. 'It's an open secret that my husband's carriage "is always at Becky's door",' says Sally Phillips, who plays Lady Steyne, 'but I think Lady Steyne accepts that society works in a certain way and this has probably happened before. Like Becky, she is probably ostracised a bit or pitied, so in a way they have common ground.'

Lady Steyne, however, cannot help Becky when Rawdon discovers her tryst with Lord Steyne, and both relationships fall apart. As Rawdon warned her, Becky has flown too high, and by entering into a pact with the likes of Lord Steyne her life is now in freefall.

Presentation at Court

THROUGH HER LIAISON with Lord Steyne, Becky achieves
what she believes is the very pinnacle of social acceptance: she and
Rawdon are presented before the King. We don't actually see the
monarch, but we are party to the build-up and the great excitement
such an event generates.

In Georgian society, presentation at Court was indeed a momentous
event for all concerned. Held at St James's Palace in London,
only the wives and daughters of peers or the landed gentry were
generally allowed to be formally presented, so Becky is something of
an anomaly. For a young woman, it marked her debut in fashionable
society and for the unmarried lady it signalled her entrée into the
marriage market.

While the actual presentation took only moments, the preparation
could take several weeks. White ostrich feathers and fine jewellery
were a must, and cream-coloured gowns with trains were favoured in
the 1820s over the hoop skirts that had been fashionable during the
reign of George III. (Becky, who is an expert at living beyond her
means, is forced to steal fabrics from Queen's Crawley for her gown.)

Extensive rules and etiquette surrounded an event at the palace and
for that reason the makers of *Vanity Fair* brought in Dr Ambrogio
Caiani to advise them on the elaborate ritual of Court presentation.
Deportment was everything and ladies would take lessons,
usually with dance instructors, to learn how to curtsy and to walk
gracefully. Accompanied by a sponsor, who was usually an older
and more established member of society, those being presented
would have a long wait outside the receiving room at St James's

Becky loved society
and, indeed, could
no more exist
without it than an
opium-eater without
his dram …

Palace, before being announced one by one.
Gentlemen would bow and ladies would normally
curtsy as they entered, then again in the middle
of the room, and once more before they kissed
the monarch's hand. A court curtsy was required,
much lower than an ordinary curtsy, bending the
knee almost to the floor, holding for a moment,
then rising again with head elegantly bowed.

As it was also considered rude to turn one's back
on a monarch, ladies and gentleman then had to
back out of the room – no mean feat in a dress
with a long train. A lady would thus have to take
hold of her train and push it to one side as she
gracefully reversed. We don't see Becky do this,
but one assumes she accomplishes it perfectly.

The age of scandal

LORD STEYNE'S ADULTERY, which his wife is simply forced to accept, is the type of dissolute behaviour that many of Thackeray's contemporaries would have expected from a period in history often labelled the age of scandal. Certainly, scandal was never far from the surface at the top level of society. George IV had been a womaniser from an early age and had a steady stream of mistresses throughout his life, providing perfect fodder for cartoonists of the day. In 1785, George, then Prince of Wales, secretly wed Maria Fitzherbert; the marriage was later claimed to be invalid. He then agreed to marry Princess Caroline of Brunswick in exchange for Parliament paying some of his debts. Predictably, the marriage was a disaster, climaxing in his failed attempt to divorce Caroline in 1820.

The King's brothers and close circle were no better; his brother the Duke of Clarence, the future William IV, had ten illegitimate children with the well-known actress Mrs Jordan.

The Prince of Wales considers his mistresses.

King William IV's mistress, Mrs Jordan.

Even the nation's military heroes were caught up in such liaisons: Nelson famously had an affair with the artist's model and actress Emma Hamilton, and the Duke of Wellington was a known womaniser; his mistress Harriette Wilson was one the most famous courtesans of the time.

In aristocratic circles, a man could survive the scandal of adultery with his reputation intact, whereas for a woman it was entirely different: she could lose her children and means of support, and end up a social outcast. Lord Steyne might have received a blow to the head from Rawdon but as a wealthy and powerful peer of the realm he is largely untouched by the affair, whereas Becky is forced to flee society and Rawdon, without power or money, is left emasculated, a broken man. Legally, a woman could not cite a husband's unfaithfulness as grounds for divorce, whereas a man could claim damages if his wife had an affair. The offence of adultery was known as 'criminal conversation' and eye-watering sums were paid by some members of the aristocracy to wronged husbands. Divorce itself was rare and expensive, requiring an Act of Parliament for formal annulment. Most husbands and wives either had to live with each other for life, or agree to an open marriage, and wives on the whole simply had to put up with their husbands' philandering.

Lord Steyne received a blow to the head from Rawdon.

The Bareacres

Becky is snubbed by various grand people at Lord Steyne's house, among them Lord and Lady Bareacres and their daughter Lady Blanche. Snooty and superior, they would rather talk amongst themselves than be demeaned by associating with the likes of Becky. In Brussels, they shun Becky, George and Amelia, although Becky gets her revenge by refusing to sell them her horses when they're desperate to flee the city.

BECKY

Lady Blanche. Lady Bareacres. Possibly you don't remember me from Brussels ...

LADY BAREACRES

I neither remember you, Madam, nor wish now to resume our intercourse.

The sponging house

Creditors finally catch up with Rawdon and he is taken by bailiffs to a sponging house. There, in this dreary den, he is greeted by the proprietor like an old friend. While he and Becky have managed remarkably well to live on nothing a year, albeit largely at the expense of local tradesmen and the faithful Crawley servants and new landlords the Raggleses, their nefarious activities are starting to get them into trouble. The sponging house was a place of temporary confinement for debtors, a private house where money was squeezed out (like a sponge) from its detainees in order to repay creditors. If debtors couldn't pay up quickly they might then be taken to court and sent to a debtors' prison.

Thackeray himself ran into financial problems and in the 1830s was forced to resort to bill-discounting, a kind of transferred debt-collecting, an activity that he largely kept to himself, but which gave him an insight into the whole system of credit and debt.

BECKY

… he's a frightful miser, as
well as the most complete
nincompoop you ever saw …

BUTE CRAWLEY

BUTE CRAWLEY HAS inherited the baronetcy of Queen's Crawley, along with Sir Pitt's estate and fortune, on the death of his father. It is Bute, played by Mathew Baynton, who stumps up the money to release Rawdon from the debtors' prison, and who takes in his son Rawdy and their devoted servant Briggs. A charitable gesture, although Bute and his disapproving wife Martha spend much of the story reproaching the behaviour of those around them: Sir Pitt's coarse ways, Rawdon's rakish London life and Becky's lowly background. From the outset, Martha, played by Sian Clifford, goes out of her way to discover the truth of Becky's parentage, and revels in the discovery that she is 'the spawn of a drunk and a harlot'. Both are deeply religious (Bute is a rector), pious and preachy – the kind of people who could suck the joy out of any room.

Bute and Martha Crawley, with Rawdy and Briggs.

BUTE

Say no. Rawdon, I beg you.

RAWDON

No wife. No home. No honour.
What else is left? It's the end of the line.

Creating the look

A KEY ELEMENT in any period drama is how individual characters are dressed and made up. Costume and hair need to fit the period, but they must also show something of the characters' own personalities, their stories and station in life. For *Vanity Fair*, teams of costume, hair and make-up designers were brought in to create the look, among them Vickie Lang, who designed hair and make-up, and Lucinda Wright and Suzie Harman who created the costumes.

To prepare for such a big production as *Vanity Fair*, those involved with costume and make-up research the period as much as possible, looking into what exactly was being worn and in fashion between the years 1813 and 1830, using contemporary paintings as references. The novel itself is also a critical resource for the team, and the designers use modern photography and magazine images to inspire them and to help create a visual palette for each scene and location. Early discussions are had with key members of the production team, including director James Strong, producer Julia Stannard and production designer Anna Pritchard, to discuss their vision and requirements, and to look at locations and background colours for each scene.

Regency style

In 1813, women's clothing was Grecian in style and corsets had been abandoned in favour of a natural and simple silhouette. Gowns were free-flowing, made in lightweight fabrics such as cotton, muslin or silk, and were at least ankle length, with a high 'empire' waist. Some bodices scooped quite low in the front, and sometimes a light, semi-transparent overdress was worn on top of the main gown. For outerwear, the spencer, a waist-length jacket, was popular, as was the fuller-length coat, the pelisse. Make-up was fairly natural-looking – gone were the days of the whitened faces of the eighteenth century – and women might have used resins and charcoals on eyebrows, and balms and beeswax on lips. It was fashionable to have hair piled high on the head in a classically inspired style, with hanging wisps and ringlets about the face.

Men's clothing was particularly stylish in the Regency period, and heavily influenced by the military. Snug-fitting breeches were becoming longer and, as popularised by dandies, eventually to be replaced by trousers. Shirts were made of linen and had high collars, with necks wrapped in stocks or cravats. These were often paired with a contrasting waistcoat and coat. Hessian boots – knee-high riding boots – remained popular, and would later evolve into the Wellington boot, as popularised by the Duke of Wellington.

Becky's look

A lot of work and thought went into the look of Becky Sharp, not only because she's the lead in *Vanity Fair* but also because her character is something of a chameleon. To get on in society, Becky reinvents herself again and again, from orphan schoolgirl to country governess, officer's wife and high-society hostess to down-at-heel exile – and each look needs to reflect that change.

CLOCKWISE FROM TOP LEFT:

At Pinkerton's, Becky, like many of her fellow pupils, wears simple dresses in soft pastel colours. Here Becky looks young and fresh, with natural-looking make-up. In other scenes she wears a ribbon in her hair, which is softly curled.

When Becky goes to Queen's Crawley as a governess she still wears simple muslin dresses, but here she has more of a gypsy look, with a headscarf and looser hair – a nod perhaps to her bohemian upbringing.

Becky starts to wear more colours and increasingly ladylike clothes as she marries Rawdon and begins to rise in society.

Becky is now mingling in high society. Her hair is more structured, adorned by accessories, and she wears expensive jewellery.

To be presented before the King, Becky has a fashionable 'Apollo knot' in her hair and extravagant ostrich feathers, and wears a beautifully embroidered cream gown and green train.

Becky has a more sultry look, with darker eyes and looser hair, and she appears a little older, but she still has sex appeal.

The dress style is now entirely different: gone are the lightweight empire-line dresses, in are heavier fabrics, puffed sleeves and skirts that billow out.

OLIVIA COOKE: Becky plays around with fashion and her look in order to make herself look a certain way: sexually appealing; or twee and virginal; harmless; authoritarian, or to look like a woman who runs a house.

OLIVIA COOKE: My favourite look was the opera in Brussels – a gorgeous deep red Grecian number, with plumes of material over my shoulders. It falls in a romantic way, with shiny silk gloves – it's just fab.

OLIVIA COOKE: In the beginning, Becky's hair is more unruly: Amelia describes it as 'wild'. And then it gets more ornate as the years go on, until she comes full circle and we see her in Pumpernickel and her hair is dishevelled. I like the dishevelled look a bit more!

Other characters

Hair and make-up designer Vickie Lang gives her insights:

AMELIA – 'Amelia's look is more innocent and naïve. Her hair was lightened to a Titian red, to give her a more romantic look. She's not so interested in her appearance so she doesn't change too much – although when she loses George she actually shears her hair off, which is quite shocking.' By the end of series Amelia looks more fashionable, in fur, with more structured hair.

RAWDON – For the Court presentation, Tom wears tight-fitting breeches and a fine embroidered waistcoat. Rawdon is usually seen in his military uniform, although the costume designer Lucinda Wright wanted him to wear civilian clothes for the debtors' prison scene. 'For men, it was fashionable to have a short haircut at time – in a classical "Titus" style. Rawdon, however, is a bit of a rebel and we didn't want to cut off Tom's lovely locks, so we kept his hair curly and fairly dishevelled, and gave it a period feel.'

GEORGE – 'George is quite vain and probably takes quite a lot of care over his appearance. For his sideburns, I wanted something that suited Charlie's face, which didn't overpower him too much. Rather than sticking his sideburns on, I laid them on, which involves taking a small clump of hair and sticking it on, bit by bit. It takes a bit of time but looks more natural.'

MATILDA – In an intimate scene, Becky helps Aunt Matilda take off her hairpiece (known as a 'front'), to reveal thin, wispy hair underneath. Matilda's hairpiece was designed so that it would deliberately look like a wig, with varying colours on show: 'Wigs at this time were often made out of your own hair collected from a brush, so I deliberately made Matilda's wig out of differently coloured bits of hair as some of it would have been her hair colour in younger days.'

DOBBIN – 'Dobbin is the light and hope in the series. We wanted to give him an understated look, attractive but not too distracting, or too constricted in the period. We wanted Dobbin and Rawdon to be very much the handsome heroes.'

JOS – 'Jos's look is eccentric and dandyish, and his facial hair changes. He's often quite sweaty and frantic, and he sports quite a big moustache in Brussels.' The costume designers had a lot of fun with Jos's wardrobe as he favours flamboyant, colourful clothes, very much influenced by India – and he is, of course, a big fan of the waistcoat!

CHAPTER
SEVEN

Endings and beginnings

I wonder, did I always know
that the prize I set my life on
was not worth winning?

THE RAGGLESES HAVE lost all their money as a result of lending their Mayfair house to Becky and Rawdon. On Lord Steyne's recommendation, Rawdon is to be made Governor-General of Coventry Island. Dobbin, in India, learns from Jos that Amelia is to marry. Mrs Sedley dies and Jos and Dobbin return to England. Dobbin confesses his love to Amelia but she cannot reciprocate. Mr Osborne dies and Amelia and Georgy, reunited, move in to the Osborne house. In the German spa town of Pumpernickel, Georgy follows a hooded lady into a gaming house, and Jos is stunned to see that the woman is Becky. Jos visits Becky in her grim tenement and she convinces him and later Amelia of her innocence. Dobbin insists that Amelia have nothing to do with Becky, but Amelia refuses and Dobbin realises she is not worthy of his love. Rawdon dies of yellow fever and Rawdy inherits Queen's Crawley. Becky tells Amelia she must marry Dobbin, and reveals the truth about George. Three years later, Dobbin and Amelia are married with a daughter, who is now the love of Dobbin's life. We end with Thackeray reminding us that none of us gets what we want in life, although we see Becky with Jos; she is undimmed, still revelling in the carousel of life, Thackeray's brilliant, mischievous creation.

Pumpernickel

WILLIAM THACKERAY, WHO, in the novel, frequently adds comments and asides, mentions that he himself saw Colonel Dobbin and his party arriving at the Erbprinz Hotel in Pumpernickel. 'Everybody remarked the majesty of Jos and the knowing way in which he sipped, or rather sucked, the Johannisberger, which he ordered for dinner.'

The narrator is of course playfully stretching the fictional conceit of the story, although his imaginary Pumpernickel (a German rye bread) is probably based on the German city of Weimar, where he spent six contented months in 1830–1. A young man at the time, Thackeray frequented the theatre, opera and Court events, dabbled in a couple of romances and enjoyed the relaxed atmosphere of the city. He took dancing lessons and even wrote home to his mother asking that she send out a militia uniform – a not-uncommon practice among gentlemen at Court, and something that perhaps finds an echo in Jos's military get-up in Brussels.

Vanity Fair is an international story, moving from London and Hampshire to Brussels, Germany and India, reflecting a world of conflict and empire, as well as a nascent global economy. These different locations also enable the narrator to place his

characters in fresh settings, and to shake up and drive forward the story. When abroad, the normal rules of life often don't apply. In Brussels, Lord and Lady Bareacres normally wouldn't associate with the likes of George and Amelia, but here they are thrown into the same social milieu. In Pumpernickel, the mores of society are relaxed and Becky can live anonymously with quite worldly people, albeit in reduced circumstances.

In addition, Becky is very much a creature of the world; she is drawn to the exciting and the exotic, and it's difficult to imagine her living within the stuffy confines of English society for too long. The very thought of India, where early on she learns Jos lives, excites her, whereas Amelia, who is far happier in the safe home environment, thinks it just sounds worryingly far away. Becky is by nature a restless character in search of the next thrill; in the novel, when she first flees England we learn she was 'very respectable and orderly at first, but the life of humdrum virtue grew utterly tedious to her before long'.

For a character like Becky, and for the vibrant, bustling world she inhabits, Thackeray creates what he sees as 'appropriate scenery … brilliantly illuminated with the Author's own candles'.

The locations

JUST AS *VANITY FAIR* zips from one place to another, so too did the series creators, who filmed in no fewer than nineteen locations in and around London, as well as in Berkshire, Kent and Budapest. As so much of *Vanity Fair* revolves around London and its society, the production team was keen to film in the capital, to bring to life the incredible metropolis of the early nineteenth century, particularly in areas where existing Georgian buildings would provide the perfect backdrop.

As a result, filming took place across the city: Princelet Street in Spitalfields was the location for some of the London street scenes, as well as the interior of the debtors' prison; Trinity Church Square in Southwark for the property leased by the Raggleses to Becky and Rawdon; Osterley House and Syon Park in Isleworth for Lord Steyne's house and Vauxhall Pleasure Gardens respectively.

Interiors were similarly shot at a variety of London locations: Lancaster House, which used to be part of St James's Palace, was used for the Court presentation scene; the Savile Club in Mayfair for the gentlemen's club scenes; Goldsmiths' Hall for Lord Steyne's party; and Marble Hill House in Twickenham for Aunt Matilda's house. Filming in a city as busy as London was obviously demanding for the production crew, added to which multiple scenes from any part of the story would be shot in each location (known as crossboarding).

Kent provided the locations for Miss Pinkerton's Academy and the Sedley cottage; a set was built at Chatham Dockyard to recreate a London shopping street; and the embarkation of troops to Waterloo was shot at Deal. The Queen's Crawley exterior scenes were filmed near Reading in Berkshire, and the Battle of Waterloo was fought on some land near by. Interiors for Queen's Crawley were filmed at West Horsley Place in Surrey.

Fitzroy Square in London's Bloomsbury was another key location, providing the setting for the Sedley and Osborne houses and various street scenes. It is one of the most beautiful Georgian squares in London and is close to both where Thackeray lived in Great Coram Street and the fictional homes of the Osbornes and Sedleys in Russell Square. Designed by the great Georgian architect Robert Adam in 1790, the houses of Fitzroy Square are some of the best surviving examples of Georgian terraced housing, although

Trinity Church Square (TOP) in Southwark and Fitzroy Square (BOTTOM) in Bloomsbury provided exterior London locations.

OPPOSITE: The beach scene, just before the elopers head to Brussels, was shot in Deal, Kent.

in the period of *Vanity Fair* the area did not match the status of London's West End. The area around Fitzroy Square was also popular with people returning from India, who invested in property there, as Jos does in the novel.

Budapest stood in for both Brussels and Pumpernickel, with filming taking place in Lion Square as well as the Royal Palace of Gödöllő, east of the city. Hungary's Baroque buildings and Germanic architecture offered a good alternative to both locations, and cobblestones provided a period feel. Vajdahunyad Castle in the Városliget Park in Budapest also made a stunning setting for Dobbin and Amelia's reunion at the end of the series.

ABOVE: Director James Strong and producer Julia Stannard.

The Gödöllő Palace stood in for the Brussels flower market, as production designer Anna Pritchard explains: 'We wanted to portray the beauty of the Brussels flower market as the troops head off to the horrors of war. I did a lot of research into flower markets of the period, looking at Dutch paintings, French tapestries and the kind of flowers they would have had at the time, from hyacinths to tulips and hydrangeas.'

LEFT, FROM TOP: Filming in Budapest city centre; Lord Steyne's party was shot at Goldsmiths' Hall in London; Chatham Dockyard, Kent.

OPPOSITE: The gaming room at Pumpernickel was filmed in a set built at Chatham Dockyard.

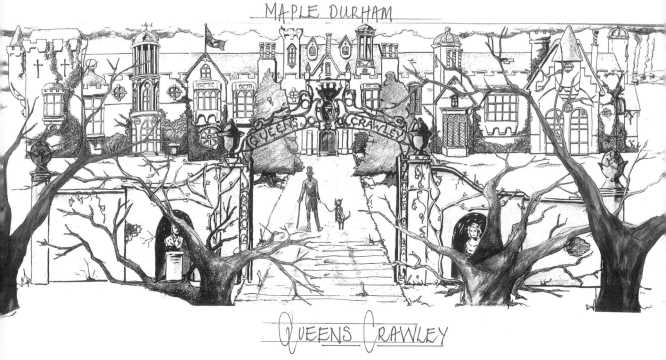

MAPLE DURHAM

QUEENS CRAWLEY

ABOVE: A production drawing for Queen's Crawley, and an image of the gates used for filming. Before locations are chosen, the director, producer, location managers and production designers discuss what they want from each setting, and design will then work up colour palettes and visual references for each location or scene.

ANNA PRITCHARD, production designer: Many of our decisions are character-driven as well: we'll talk about a particular family, where they sit in society, what size house they have, before we decide on a location. We have to do a lot of research into how houses looked two hundred years ago, and to recreate the world of *Vanity Fair* in a visual sense.

The hooded lady

She became a perfect bohemian ere long, herding with people whom it would make your hair stand on end to meet.

FOUR YEARS LATER, Becky suddenly appears as a hooded lady scurrying along the streets of Pumpernickel. Affecting a French accent, she is a regular at seedy gaming halls and now lives in a grim tenement building, just about scraping a living by dubious means.

She has indeed sunk low, falling from high-society life in England, where she was even presented at Court, to a shadowy and lonely existence in Germany. By allowing herself to be seduced by Lord Steyne and by neglecting her husband Rawdon, she is now spurned by English society and forced to live abroad. Her treacherous behaviour left Rawdon heartbroken, and exposed her as the kind of woman who could not love even her own son, as Rawdon sums up: 'Mother is the name for God in the minds of little children. And my boy worships a stone. Or he did. He got over it. We both got over it.' Becky's selfish actions left her faithful servants and landlords, the Raggleses, penniless, her son without a mother and her husband feeling he had no option other than to take up the governorship of mosquito-infested Coventry Island, where he would later die feverishly uttering her name.

'I think Becky did love Rawdon,' says Olivia Cooke, 'but she was just blinded by the fact that they didn't have any money. Becky felt she had to be the brains of the relationship. When they have a baby she can't bond with the child as much as Rawdon does, and that holds a mirror up to Becky's faults – and she doesn't like it. That's when their relationship began to break down.'

With her life in tatters, Becky is forced to pick herself up and start again, as she does repeatedly in *Vanity Fair*; she is nothing if not resilient. 'I think it takes a lot of brain power, self-motivation and desperation to propel herself again and again,' says Olivia. 'She does think of herself as a bit of a hustler, and she's forced to live the way she does to make ends meet.'

Becky's heart, scarred and buried as it is, does surface in Pumpernickel. 'I think she's genuinely pleased to see Amelia,' says Olivia, 'but she can see how much she has suffered and how she is wasting her life mourning her dead husband. She also knows how much Dobbin has cared for, loved and protected Amelia and her son.'

Becky and Amelia are reunited in Pumpernickel.

As a result, Becky does everything she can to reveal the full extent of George's infidelity, to open Amelia's eyes to just how deserving Dobbin is of her love: 'If I can persuade you to marry the Major, well, in my whole life that's my one good deed done.' Her intentions are for once selfless, and she's excited by the prospect of a happy ending for the couple.

A woman of brains and talent

Becky's good deed does show that she is not entirely without heart. While Becky is mischievous and ruthlessly ambitious, she is human and moved – if not a little frustrated – by the unending sufferings of Dobbin and Amelia. Becky is not a saint but she is an exhilarating character, who shines bright. Her soul may be 'black with vanity', as Martha Crawley puts it, but life would certainly be more boring without her. Becky starts with little and propels herself into the world, determined that nothing will stand in her way as

she climbs the ranks of English society. She believes she can succeed because she has 'brains and talent', which she could no doubt do in today's world, but, as Lady Steyne reminds her, this is the iniquitous world of *Vanity Fair*.

A woman like Becky, without money or family support, has few options if she wants to get on in life: she either has to marry well, conform and live a life of passive obedience; or she can rebel, break a few rules and use every weapon in her armoury for her advancement. Becky, a woman of spirit and fierce intelligence, chooses the latter. Right from the outset, she is wicked and defiant, from flinging her school dictionary out of her carriage to artfully charming anyone who can get her on the next rung of the social ladder. As Olivia Cooke explains: 'She thinks of herself and fights for herself. She has to because no one else is going to look out for her. In doing so, she's quite free with her sexuality, her view on commitment is quite abstract, and the way she manipulates and charms people for their money and status is shocking. She's quite unapologetic about that.'

At the same time, Becky does get things wrong, and like many characters in *Vanity Fair* makes mistakes. She succeeds in charming the wealthy Matilda Crawley, but then entirely misreads her after she marries Rawdon. Like a child, she constantly wants more and more and never knows when to stop, until she meets her nemesis in the form of Lord Steyne. 'It would be wrong to think of Becky Sharp as very organised,' says series writer Gwyneth Hughes, 'as she makes it up day by day and she gets it wrong. Young people get it wrong all the time!'

In creating the character of Becky, William Thackeray clearly admired the kind of woman Becky represented. Some have

suggested he based her on a woman named Pauline, whom he met and probably had an affair with as a young man in Paris. A former governess from a respectable family in England, Pauline had chosen the independent life, and when Thackeray met her lived in a shabby apartment in the city, not unlike that of Becky in Pumpernickel.

Whether or not Thackeray based Becky on Pauline, he certainly retained a fascination and liking for the bohemian life, and for resourceful, out-of-the-ordinary women. He himself was drawn to life abroad, was bored at times by domesticity, enjoyed high society but also engaged in the seedier side of life, knew about poverty and had to work hard to earn money and social acceptance. Thackeray wrote that, had he had a substantial annual income, he would have led a far more sober life, a belief Becky shares, saying 'I could be good. I could be very good on five thousand a year.' She, like her creator, is a product of her circumstances and Thackeray saw much of himself in Becky.

Thackeray

At the same time, Thackeray, like many Victorians, admired female modesty and purity, falling in love and marrying the 'nice, simple, girlish' Isabella Shawe, when she was just seventeen, and finding such virtues in Jane Brookfield, with whom he fell in love later in life. In this way, the sweet, virtuous and affectionate Amelia represents the more dutiful, maternal ideal of womanhood that Thackeray found appealing, describing Amelia in the novel: 'I think it was her weakness which was her principal charm – a kind of sweet submission and softness, which seemed to appeal to each man she met for his sympathy and protection.' Becky is the polar opposite: she is not virtuous, nor in any way motherly, she's certainly not timid, although she feigns tears and vulnerability as a cover for her guile.

By this means, the brilliantly drawn characters of Amelia and Becky represent two very different women, both of whom we might admire or delight in, but for very different reasons. As Olivia Cooke says: 'I hope that what people take away from *Vanity Fair* is that there's no right way to be a woman. Just as Amelia is pure and virtuous, living like a martyr and sobbing over the loss of her husband, that's not the right way to behave. At the opposite end of the spectrum, Becky is selfish, she thinks of herself and lives a life of gluttony – that's not necessarily the way to live either. These are just women trying to survive, making it up as they go along.'

MAIN CAST

Thackeray **Michael Palin**

Becky Sharp **Olivia Cooke**

Amelia Sedley **Claudia Jessie**

Rawdon Crawley **Tom Bateman**

William Dobbin **Johnny Flynn**

George Osborne **Charlie Rowe**

Jos Sedley **David Fynn**

Mr Sedley **Simon Russell Beale**

Mrs Sedley **Claire Skinner**

Sam **Richie Campbell**

Sir Pitt Crawley **Martin Clunes**

Lady Crawley **Madeleine Hyland**

Matilda Crawley **Frances de la Tour**

Bute Crawley **Mathew Baynton**

Martha Crawley **Sian Clifford**

Horrocks **Mike Grady**

Mr Osborne **Robert Pugh**

Mrs O'Dowd **Monica Dolan**

Major O'Dowd **Patrick Fitzsymons**

Lord Steyne **Anthony Head**

Lady Steyne **Sally Phillips**

Miss Pinkerton **Suranne Jones**

Jemima Pinkerton **Kerry Gilbert**

General Tufto **Richard Dixon**

Ensign Stubbs **Jack Loxton**

Reverend Binny **Oliver Lansley**

Lady Bareacres **Elizabeth Berrington**

Lord Bareacres **Will Barton**

Lady Blanche **Lily Lesser**

Isidor **Philip Desmeules**

Rhoda Swartz **Siena Kelly**

Raggles **Peter Wight**

Mrs Raggles **Maggie Daniels**

Betsey Horrocks **Lauren Crace**

ACKNOWLEDGEMENTS

A huge thank you to Megan Ott at Mammoth Screen who was my lifeline during the writing of this book, providing much-needed material and answers to all my random queries with lightning-quick speed. Many thanks also to Sven Arnstein at Stay Still Productions, whose interviews with the cast and crew of *Vanity Fair* provided a vital source for the book. At Sphere, many thanks to Adam Strange for wisely initiating the book and giving me the opportunity to be involved (it's been a joy) and to Zoe Gullen for her editorial expertise and support. A big thank you also to Sian Rance at D.R. ink for her sublime design skills and calmness under pressure.

My thanks to the hugely talented production team at Mammoth Screen for their invaluable help and allowing me to write about their world: Gwyneth Hughes, Julia Stannard, James Strong and James Gandhi. Thank you also to Lucinda Wright, Vickie Lang, Paul Biddiss, Anna Pritchard and James Penny. I am very grateful for the historical expertise and guidance of Dr Oskar Cox Jensen and Dr Ambrogio A. Caiani. At ITV, many thanks to Shirley Patton, Laura-Louise Watts, Hannah Gray and Natasha Bayford, and to Patrick Smith who provided us with the wonderful production images in the book.

PICTURE CREDITS